THE
BEADED
GARDEN

Claire Bischoff (left) and Diane Fitzgerald

*To Claire, my wonderful daughter,
for the many happy hours of
beading we've spent together.*

*My heartfelt thanks to Linda Ligon,
Judith Durant, Paulette Livers,
and everyone at Interweave Press
for their work in bringing this
book to print.*

THE
BEADED
GARDEN

*Creating Flowers
with
Beads and Thread*

DIANE FITZGERALD

Project Editor: Judith Durant
Technical Editor: Bonnie Brooks
Design and production: Paulette Livers
Illustrator: Sara Boore
Photographer: Joe Coca, except as noted
Proofreader: Nancy Arndt

INTERWEAVE PRESS

Interweave Press, Inc.
201 East Fourth Street
Loveland, Colorado 80537-5655
www.interweave.com

Printed in China through Asia Pacific Offset

Library of Congress Cataloging-in-Publication Data
Fitzgerald, Diane.
  The beaded garden : creating flowers with beads and thread / Diane Fitzgerald.
      p. cm.
  Includes bibliographical references and index.
  ISBN 1-931499-55-1
  1. Bead flowers. I. Title.
  TT890.2.F58 2005
  745.58'2—dc22
                                                    2005006238

10 9 8 7 6 5 4 3 2 1

SEVENTEENTH CENTURY STUART BASKET

Baskets like these may have been made to celebrate betrothal and used to hold gloves or sprigs of rosemary given to wedding guests. One of two similar baskets in the Burrell Collection, the frame is wrapped with strands of beads, beaded fruit, flowers, and leaves attached to the frame and worked in double-needle right-angle weave. The basket is part of the Burrell Collection of the Glasgow Museums, Scotland. Size 50 X 63 cm.

CONTENTS

Welcome to My Garden

For hundreds of years, flower lovers have been creating blossoms out of almost every conceivable material: paper, fabric, gemstones, metal, leather, bread, hair, feathers, shells, pearls, ribbon, cake frosting, and of course, beads and wire. In this book, we'll continue this tradition, but with a new approach: We'll explore the craft of making flowers with tiny glass beads and *thread*, weaving these elements together with off-loom stitches to create three-dimensional flowers, leaves, and garden creatures.

In creating a flower with any kind of material, one can only hope to approximate the delicate, fragile qualities of a natural bloom. While some details may need to be omitted entirely, others may only be suggested. Imitating the exquisite color shading and three-dimensional shapes is a goal that we'll strive toward but rarely achieve with the true subtlety of Mother Nature. In pursuing this humbling experience we will gain knowledge about flowers and come to appreciate their beauty and complexity more than we ever did before. We may also begin to see why throughout time flowers have been so loved and admired. Ultimately, our glass bead flowers should be appreciated for themselves: They may get dusty, but their bloom will not fade or wilt.

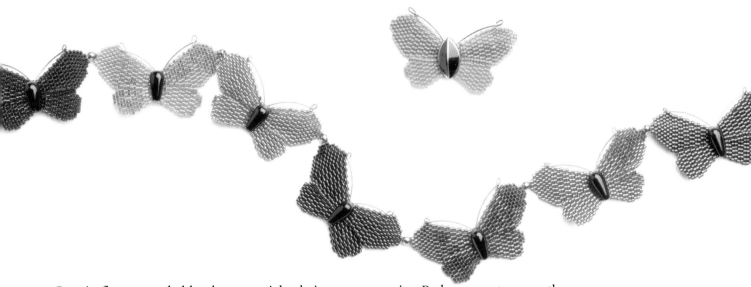

Certain flowers probably play a special role in our memories. Perhaps you treasure the flowers you carried at your wedding, the dozen long-stemmed red roses you received on Valentine's Day, or the corsage you wore to the prom. As a child, did you make dolls from hollyhocks or pinch snapdragons to see them open and close? My most cherished flower memories are of the white and red peonies my mother tended so carefully, the wild yellow roses in my grandmother's garden, and of my daughter (who had never strung a bead) learning to do beadwork because she wanted a Scottish Thistle!

I hope this book will inspire you and provide you with many hours of pleasure as you create your own beaded garden.

Diane M. Fitzgerald

P.S. You may reach me through www.dianefitzgerald.com.

FLOWER BASICS

SIMPLIFIED FLOWER ANATOMY

Flowers are the reproductive parts of many plants. In the center of the petals we find the stamen and the pistil. Under the petals we find the calyx and the stem.

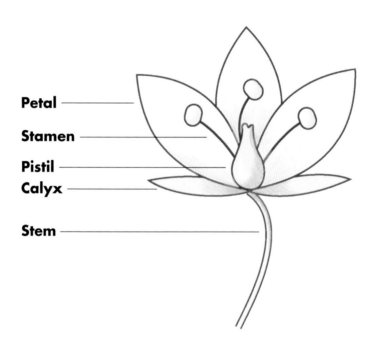

Petal
Stamen
Pistil
Calyx
Stem

"Earth laughs in flowers."
—Ralph Waldo Emerson

SOME NOTES ON CONSTRUCTING FLOWERS

As you work with the designs in this book, you will find that the directions enable you to make the basic shapes of many flowers. Petals and leaves may be oval and tapered, round, long and narrow, ruffled, pointed, or other shapes. Enlarging or reducing the size of a particular petal or leaf may be the beginning of a flower you wish to create. Also, many parts can be combined to form other natural flowers or new fantasy flowers.

Flower Centers

An integral part of every flower is its center or stamen and pistils. The center provides a focal point and a base on which to attach petals and, if you decide to include them, the calyx and stem. Here are some bases that can be used for flower centers:

• fabric-covered button (Dritz Half Ball Cover Buttons are recommended)
• foam ball or half-ball covered with fabric, yarn, or thread
• felted ball or half-ball
• Netted Bead, an Easy Beaded Bead (instructions on page 36), or bead covered in peyote stitch
• Christmas tree lightbulb, pointed or round
• button sewed to a small circle of stiff nonwoven interfacing material
• circle of fabric stuffed with felt or cotton and covered with beads

Petals

Petals can be shaped with any stitch and by increasing or decreasing to give the petal a flat or three-dimensional shape. I prefer brick, peyote, and square stitches because each offers unique shaping possibilities. Netting and right-angle weave work, too, but they are usually open stitches that produce a lacier texture than brick, peyote, and square stitches do.

Leaves

Most flowers have leaves, often in some shade of green, which serve as a backdrop for flowers. In addition to making beaded leaves, consider using silk leaves for beaded flowers. Trim a large silk leaf to obtain the shape needed for a particular flower.

Stems

If you want a flower to be self-supporting with a stem, you may use wrapped floral stem wire available in the artificial flower section of craft stores. The 18-gauge wrapped wire supports most flowers; use 22-gauge for small flowers. The 18" (46 cm) long straight wire is preferable to wire on a spool because it won't have kinks.

Attaching Floral Stem Wire to a Flower or Bead

A wood, glass, or plastic bead can serve as a stamen and offer a way to attach a flower to a stem wire. If the hole is larger than the stem wire, wrap the end of the wire with sewing thread until it fits snugly inside the bead. Remove the wrapped end and coat it with white glue and insert in the bead again. Allow the glue to dry. Now pass the stem through the hole in the bottom of the flower, add a sequin or flat bead and a drop of white glue below the sequin, and wrap the stem with more thread just below the sequin. You may also stitch beads at the bottom of the flower to the wrapped thread to hold the flower in place.

Stiffening Flowers

Sometimes you may want flowers to hold their shape or you may wish to shape them in a certain way. Beadwork can be stiffened just like fabric with starch by dipping it in Future Acrylic Floor Wax. Place the liquid wax in a small plastic container and dip the flower. Shake off the excess wax onto a paper towel or rag and pour the remaining wax back in the bottle. Let the flower dry for about 24 hours. If the flower contains dyed or color-lined beads, dip it quickly—just in and out. The color on these beads can bleed to other beads and create unwanted effects. On the other hand, a little experimenting may lead you to some interesting blends.

TOOLS

Needles

Most experienced beaders have a favorite type of needle. Some like beading needles, which are 2" (5 cm) long; others prefer Sharps, which are 1.25" (3.2 cm) long. A few prefer Big Eye needles for ease of threading; surprisingly, they will go through many size 11° seed beads, but not as often as a thinner needle. I encourage people to use the type of needle they prefer and, if it won't go through beads the required number of times, to switch to a thinner needle. Size 10 needles are thicker than size 11 or 12. If you are using Japanese seed beads or cylinder beads (Delicas, Treasures, or Aikos) you will be able to use a size 10 needle almost all the time. If you are using Czech seed beads, you will need a size 12 needle because the holes in these beads are smaller and somewhat irregular.

Thread

I recommend Nymo D or C-Lon threads for all the flowers in this book. Both are strong, durable threads and available in many colors. Some beaders prefer Silamide or Fireline (6 lb or 4 lb). Silamide is a twisted nylon thread that's also available in several colors. Fireline is a stiff nylon thread similar to fishing line and is available only in gray. Thread color is important because it affects bead color.

ADDING NEW THREAD This method of changing thread works well for most projects. It's quick and easy, and the two knots make a secure join. When you have about 4" (10 cm) of thread left, leave the needle on the old thread. Thread a new needle and knot the end. Clip the tail close to the knot (about ¹⁄₁₆" [.16 cm] or less) and melt the tail slightly with a lighter. Melting the end of the thread prevents little fuzzies from showing and fuses the knot, which will slip inside a bead. Bring the needle through 4 to 6 beads so the thread is exiting the same bead as the old thread and in the same direction. Tie the old thread to the new thread with a square knot (see page 108). Bring the old thread (with the needle still on it) through 4 to 6 beads and clip close to the beads. Dab the knot with clear nail polish. You're all set to keep beading!

WAXING AND WORKING WITH DOUBLE THREAD For durability or stiffness, some designs call for a double thread that is well waxed. The wax is necessary to help control the thread and prevent knotting and needless frustration. I prefer to use synthetic or composition wax (the kind that comes in a small plastic cup) because it stays somewhat soft and sticky for several years without drying out like beeswax. Cut the required length of thread and thread it in the needle. Bring the ends together and knot. Wrap the thread at the knot end around your left forefinger and, holding the cup in your right hand, draw the wax along the thread in short strokes. Be sure the two strands are touching each other as you draw them through. Finally, draw the thread between your fingers to remove excess wax.

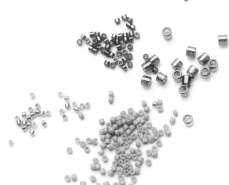

Cylinder beads are like little tubes.

MELTING THE THREAD TAILS NEAR THE KNOT To avoid fuzzy ends in your work and to secure knots in the end of thread, I melt the ends with a lighter. If you're unfamiliar with using a lighter, first practice pushing the lever and holding it down. Then hold the lighter in your dominant hand and the thread in your nondominant hand with no more than ½" (1.25 cm) extending beyond your fingers. Brace the fingers of your nondominant hand against your dominant hand and very slowly move the thread tails toward the base of the flame. Withdraw the thread when it begins to melt slightly. The thread should not flame or make a dark unsightly knot. If it does, try again—but don't bring the knot so close to the flame.

Beads

I use seed beads and cylinder beads for most of the flowers in this book. Seed beads are round and have thicker walls than cylinder beads. Cylinder beads

Toho Aiko beads' dimensions are perfectly consistent.

Seed beads are round and have thicker walls than cylinder beads.

are like little tubes. I recommend Japanese seed beads because they are more uniform and have larger holes than Czech seed beads. Cylinder beads, which some refer to as Delicas, are made by two Japanese companies: The Miyuki Company makes Delicas and the Toho Company makes Treasures and Aikos. Aikos are noted for their near-perfect uniformity.

Holding Beadwork

If you are an experienced beader, you may have developed your own style of holding work. If you are new to beadwork, here are some suggestions that may help. I hold my work between the thumb and forefinger of my left (nondominant) hand with the working thread wrapped over my forefinger and held in place with my middle finger. I hold the tail with my little finger. As I work with my right (dominant) hand, I move my thumb back slightly to expose the work. This method allows me to control the tension and to easily see which bead the thread is exiting. For brick stitch I work left to right; for peyote stitch and netting, back and forth; and for square stitch, right to left.

STAMEN

This stamen can be made with the beads suggested in the supply list and many others.

Materials

8 cylinder beads (Delicas, Treasures, or Aikos)

28 size 14° seed beads

4 size 6° or 8° seed beads

Step 1. Thread a needle with ¾ yd (68.5 cm) of single thread and make a base row with cylinder beads 2 beads tall and 4 beads long according to the instructions for Brick Stitch Base Row on page 104. If desired and depending on the size of the flower, add two more columns of beads for a total of six.

Step 2. Add a strand of fringe with 6 size 14° seed beads, 1 size 6° or 8°, and 1 size 14°. Then, skipping the last size 14°, go back through all these beads and into the 2 beads of the base (Figure 1). Come up through the next 2 beads in the base and repeat this step for each column of beads in the base.

Step 3. Join the ends of the base row and sew the stamen to the flower center or, if the flower will have a stem, wrap the end of the stem wire with thread and glue the stamen to the wire (Figure 2).

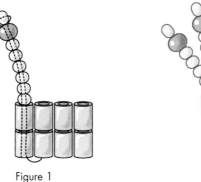

Figure 1   Figure 2

"And I will make thee beds of roses And a thousand fragrant posies."
—*Christopher Marlowe*

BULBOUS STAMEN

Materials

18-gauge wrapped stem wire
6 x 1" (15 x 2.5 cm) piece of T-shirt material
Seed beads of your choice
White glue

Step 1. Put a dab of white glue on the end of the flower stem wire. Fold the T-shirt material in half lengthwise and wrap it around the wire. Begin by folding ½" (1.3 cm) of the strip over the end of the wire, then wrap around the wire so that it forms a bulbous shape, usually 1 to 1 ½" (2.5 to 3.8 cm) long, but whatever shape or length you wish. Secure the fabric by wrapping with thread and sewing the thread into the fabric at the end so that it holds the wrap in place (Figure 1).

Step 2. Stitch a ring of seed beads to the bottom of the wrap. From these beads work tubular peyote stitch toward the tip, increasing as necessary by adding 2 beads in place of 1. When you near the tip, begin to decrease by replacing the pairs of beads with one bead. Pass the thread through the last 3–5 beads and pull tight to end off the tip. Knot the thread and weave in the tail. (See Peyote Stitch Basics on page 106.)

"From Sweet April showers
Do spring May Flowers."
—*Thomas Tusser*

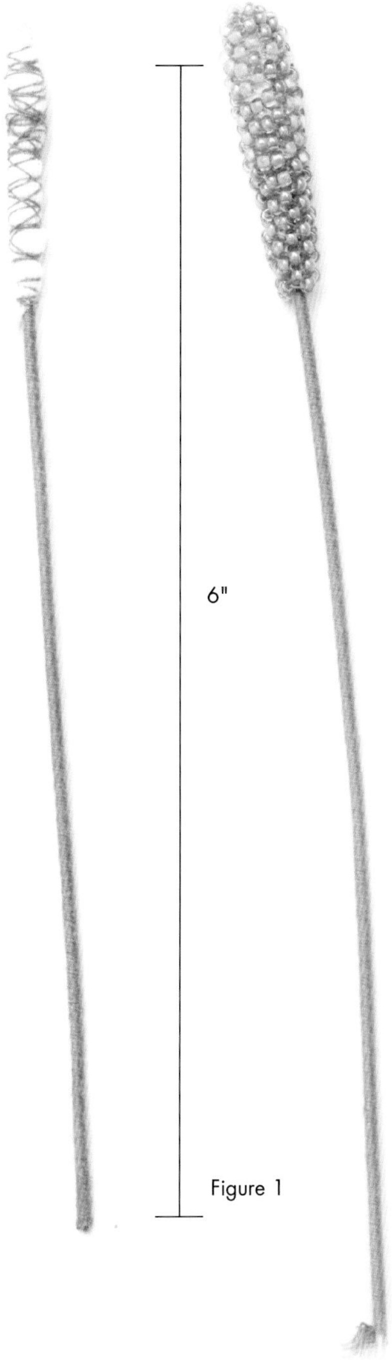

6"

Figure 1

17

ROUND DOMED STAMEN

Materials

1 Dritz Half Ball Cover Button, any size
Piece of T-shirt material, enough to cover button
Size 11° and 14° seed beads

Cover the button with fabric according to the manufacturer's instructions. Anchor 1 yd (91.5 cm) of thread in the center of the button and stitch beads one at a time to the surface so that the beads lie on their side. Add short strands of fringe around the edge of the button (Figure 1). Another method is to add a size 11° seed bead and a size 14° seed bead and go back through the 11° and into the fabric. For both methods, leave the side edge free so that petals may be added to the stamen.

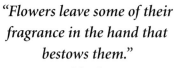

Figure 1

"Flowers leave some of their fragrance in the hand that bestows them."
—*Old Chinese Proverb*

STAMEN FROM ARTIFICIAL FLOWERS

Remove the stamen from an artificial flower and attach it to a beaded flower with thread or glue. You may also purchase artificial stamens at a craft store.

BEADED STEM

Work tubular peyote stitch over a piece of wrapped 18-gauge stem wire using size 14/15° seed beads. Begin with a ring of 7 beads and work odd-count tubular peyote (see page 106). To finish the ends, go through the 3 beads that are sticking up at the ends of the tube, knot, and weave in the tail. Sew the stem to the flower and sew leaves to the stem.

CALYX

This calyx pattern is recreated from a flower in a beaded necklace from Saraguro, Ecuador. It may also be used as a flower.

Materials

2 g size 11° seed beads or cylinder beads

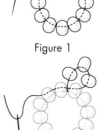

Figure 1

Row 1: Thread a needle with 1½ yd (137 cm) of single thread, string on 12 beads and tie to form a ring (Figure 1).

Row 2: Make the first picot: Pick up 3 beads and go right to left through the bead to the right of the knot and through the next 2 beads to the left (Figure 2). Make five more picots to complete this round, but on the last picot, go through only 1 bead to the left and then through the first bead of the first picot (Figure 3).

Figure 2

Row 3: Add 1 bead and go into the tip bead of the first picot. Add 3 beads and go through the tip bead of the picot again from right to left. Add 1 bead and go through the third bead of the picot. Go through the first bead of the next picot (Figure 4). Repeat this step five more times, ending by going through the first bead of the first picot in Row 2, then through the 2 beads above it.

Figure 3

Row 4: Add 1 bead, go into the tip bead of the picot in Row 3, then continue adding picots to each picot as before, but add 1 bead between each spoke and go into the first bead of the Row 3 picot (Figure 5). Keep tension tight so the piece forms a cup.

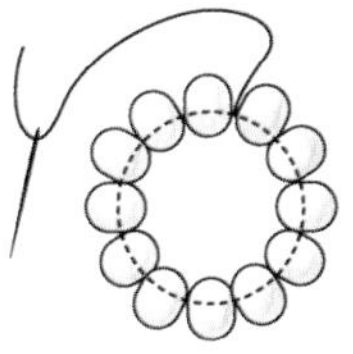

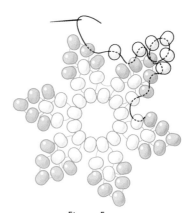

Figure 4

Figure 5

Figure 1

Figure 2

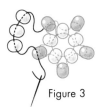

Figure 3

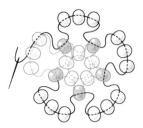

Figure 4

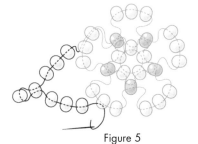

Figure 5

FLAT CALYX

A five-point flat calyx will work well for some flowers. It can be made in various sizes.

Materials

3 g size 11° seed beads

Smaller Flat Calyx

Row 1: Thread a needle with ¾ yd (68.5 cm) single thread, add 5 beads, and tie in a ring leaving a 3" (7.5 cm) tail (Figure 1).

Row 2: Add 1 bead and go into the next bead (do not skip a bead). Repeat four more times. Go through the first bead of this row (Figure 2). Going through the first bead is the "jump up," which puts the needle in the proper position to begin the next row.

Row 3: Add 3 beads and go into the next bead added in Row 2 (Figure 3). Repeat four more times. Go through the first 2 beads of the first set of 3 added in this row (Figure 4).

Row 4: Add 5 beads. Go back through the next-to-last bead. Add 3 beads. Go into the middle bead of the next set of 3 added in the previous row (Figure 5). Repeat this step four more times. Knot the thread and weave in the tails.

Larger Flat Calyx

Work Rows 1–3 as for Smaller Flat Calyx.

Row 4: Add 5 beads and go into the middle bead of the next set of 3 added in the previous row. Repeat four more times. Go through the first 3 beads of the first set of 5 added in this row.

Row 5: Add 7 beads and go into the middle bead of the next set of 5 added in the previous row. Repeat four more times. Go through the first 4 beads of the first set of 7 added in this row.

Row 6: Add 7 beads. Go back through the next-to-last bead. Add 5 beads. Go into the middle bead of the next set of 7 added in the previous row. Repeat this step four more times. Knot the thread and weave in the tails.

*"Nature is painting for us,
day after day, pictures of
infinite beauty."*
—John Ruskin

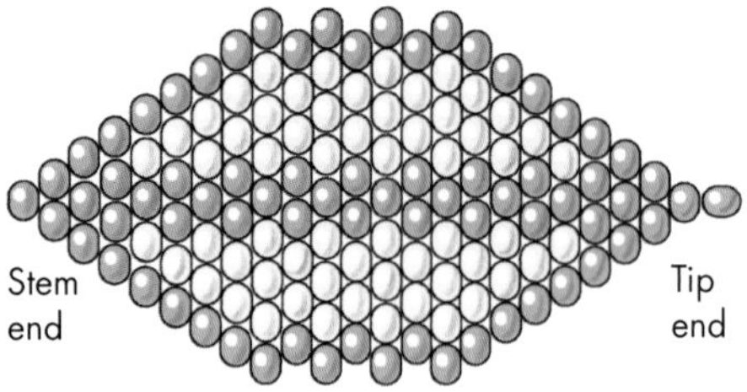

Stem end   Tip end

Note: To simplify these illustrations, fewer beads are shown than are called for.

Figure 1

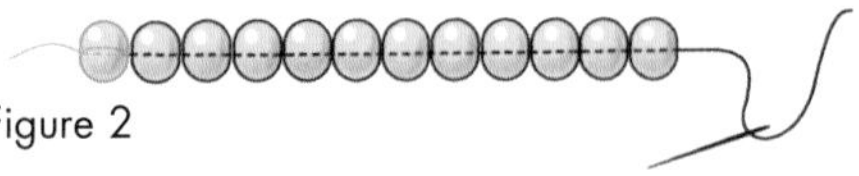

Figure 2

Figure 3

Figure 4

Figure 5

OVAL PETALS OR LEAVES

By working first along one side of the center spine and then the other, you can make many flowers with basic petals or leaf shapes formed with seed or cylinder beads and peyote stitch. As you will see, they may be made in any size and may be varied in several ways to represent many types of petals and leaves.

Materials

About 4 g seed or cylinder beads in any size; amount will vary with size of leaf

Thread a needle with 1 to 1½ yd (137 cm) of single thread and tie 1 bead on the end of the thread (this bead will be left in the work) leaving a 3–4" (8–10 cm) tail (Figure 1). To form the spine, string on 21 more beads (Figure 2). (The leaf may be made any length but begin with an *even* number of beads total.) Go back through the next-to-last bead strung, forming the tip end (Figure 3).

Work peyote stitch toward the stem end as follows: Add 1 bead and go into the second bead along the strand counting from where the thread exited a bead. Continue in this manner to the end of the row. End exiting the tied-on bead (Figure 4). Turn and, without adding a bead, go into the last bead added.

Work back and forth across the row in peyote stitch as described above; at the end of each row, turn and, without adding a bead, go into the last bead added (Figure 5). Work until there are 4 beads "sticking up" on one side of the leaf (or the desired number of rows). Pass the thread through the beads to the end of the spine and exit the second bead from the stem end on the other side of the spine with the thread pointing toward the tip end. Work along the spine on the other side in the same manner. Knot the thread and weave in the tails.

Variations

1. SHAPED LEAVES To make shaped leaves, use Delicas for the spine (first row strung on), the first row of peyote on the first side of the spine, the first and last bead of each row, and the last two rows on each side.
   Use size 11° seed beads for the rest of the leaf.
   Use double thread and wax well. Keep tension tight.

Shaped leaf

2. TWO-COLOR LEAVES Make the spine of the leaf and the first row of peyote on one side in one color. Use the same color for the first and last bead of each row and the last two rows on each side. Work the remaining beads in a second color. If desired, add 1 or 2 odd-colored beads to the leaf as highlights or leaf mold.

Five-petal flower made vith Variation One, Shaped Leaves. Petals are joined with square stitch. (See *Joining Edges with Square Stitch* on page 108.)

3. PETALS OR LEAVES WITH SERRATED EDGES When you're turning at the end of a row and before you begin a new row, instead of skipping the bead just exited and then going through the last bead added, add a size 14° seed bead and go back through the bead just exited and the last bead added to begin a new row (Figure 1).

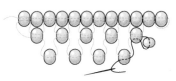

Figure 1

Serrated edge petal or leaf

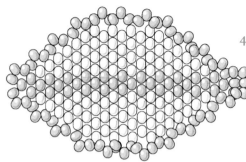

Figure 2

4. PETALS OR LEAVES WITH RUFFLED EDGES Add 3-bead loops between every other bead around the edge of the leaf with size 11° seed beads (Figure 2).

Leaves with Ruffled
Edge joined to form
coleus leaves

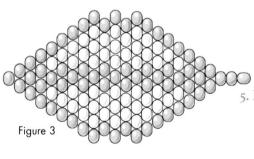

Figure 3

Figure 4

5. PETALS OR LEAVES WITH LONGER, MORE POINTED TIPS Add 1 extra bead to the spine (begin with an *uneven* total number of beads instead of an even number), then go back through 2 beads instead of 1 at the tip end on the first row of the leaf (Figures 3 and 4).

6. **Curved Petals or Leaves** Add beads for the spine row and work back to the beginning. On the next row, increase once in the middle by adding 2 beads instead of 1 (Figure 5). Continue to add 2 beads above the 2 for the rest of this side. On the other side of the leaf, decrease 1 bead in the middle by skipping a bead. On the next row, add 2 beads where you skipped a bead. On the next row, go through the 2 beads. On the next row, add only 1 bead instead of 2 at the decrease (Figure 6).

Figure 5

Figure 6

7. **Compound Leaf** Make three or five leaves and join with square stitch (see Joining Edges with Square Stitch on page 108) along the lower diagonal edges (Figures 7 and 8). Add a square stitch stem as described for the Morning Glory on page 61.

Figure 7

Figure 8

Simply Leaves
Oval Petals or Leaves are made and then strung separated by a small round bead.

Ruffled Leaves Necklace
Flowers assembled with five to
seven Oval Petals or Leaves,
Variation Four, then joined to form
a necklace with a snap closure.

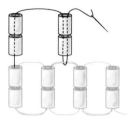

Figure 1

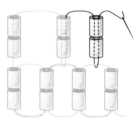

Figure 2

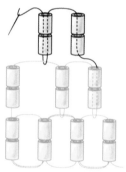

Figure 3

These leaves are made with a combination of brick stitch and square stitch. Cylinder beads are suggested, but you could also use seed beads.

Materials

2 g cylinder beads

Step 1. Thread needle with 1½ yd (137 cm) of single thread. Make a brick-stitch base 2 beads high and four columns wide as described in Brick Stitch Basics on page 104.

Step 2. With thread exiting on the left, add 4 beads, then catch the thread between the second and third columns and go back through the last 2 beads (Figure 1). Add 2 beads, then catch the thread between the third and fourth columns of the previous row and go back through the last 2 beads (Figure 2). You have now decreased from four columns to three.

Step 3. Add 4 beads, then catch the thread between the second and third columns and go back through the last 2 beads (Figure 3). Lock the stitch as described in Brick Stitch Basics on page 105. You have now decreased to two columns of beads.

Step 4. Now we'll switch to square stitch: Add 2 beads, go down through 2 beads in the last row and up through the 2 beads next to them and the first new bead added (Figure 4). Continue this step until the blade is the desired length, usually about twelve rows.

Step 5. To make the point, add 5 beads. Skipping the last bead, come back through 4 beads and continue down the column next to the one the thread exited. Knot the thread and weave in the tail (Figure 5).

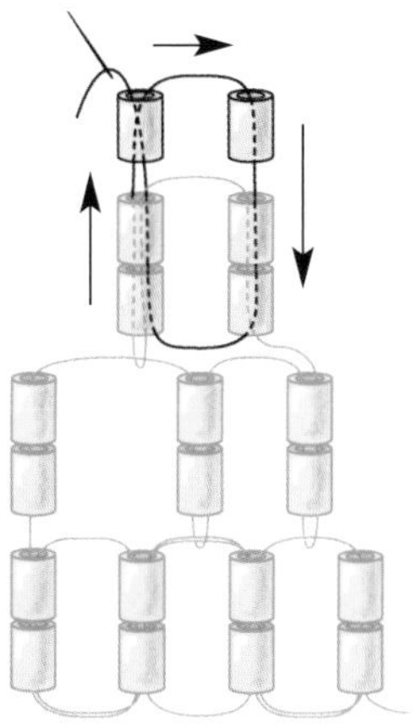

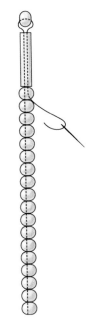

Figure 4 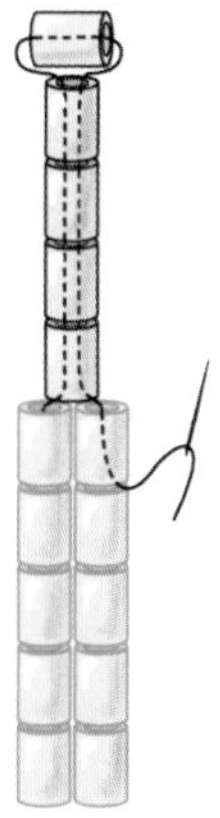   Figure 5

PALM LEAF

My thanks to Alois Powers for creating and sharing this leaf. It has many possibilities for easy shaping as a curved leaf, a twisted leaf, or a straight, flat leaf. Make one as described here and then make another, changing it as you wish.

Materials
21 size 4 bugle beads (10mm)
15 g size 11° seed beads

Note: To simplify the illustrations, fewer beads are shown than are called for.

Step 1. Thread a needle with 2 yd (183 cm) of thread, bring the ends together and knot with an overhand knot. Tie on 1 seed bead using the Lark's Head Knot Beginning instructions for a single bead on page 107. (This bead will be left in the work.) For the main stem, string on 24 more seed beads, 1 bugle, and 1 seed bead. Skipping the last seed bead strung, go back through the bugle and 1 seed bead (Figure 1).

Figure 1

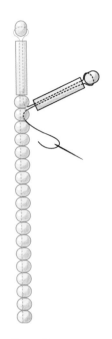

Figure 2

Step 2. Add 1 bugle and 1 seed bead, go back through the bugle bead and then through the next seed bead on the main stem (Figure 2). Continue to add 1 bugle and 1 seed bead in this manner until there are 4 beads left on the main stem. Go through these 4 beads.

Leaf Edge

Add 8 seed beads and go through the seed bead at the tip of the first bugle/seed going up the stem. Add 1 seed bead and, skipping the next bugle/seed (leaving it for the other side), go into the third one. Continue to work up the stem, connecting every other bugle/seed (Figure 3).

When you have connected the last bugle/seed, add 4 beads and go into the tip bead of the leaf (the one at the end of the bugle on the main stem), then add 4 more beads and begin connecting the bugle/seeds on the other side of the leaf. Add 3 seed beads and go into the next bugle/seed, then add 2 seed beads and go into the next bugle/seed. Continue to alternate 3 and 2 beads between bugle/seed to make the leaf curve slightly. After the last one, add 8 beads and go into the very first bead strung. Knot the thread and weave in the tail.

Variations

For a twisted leaf, add 3 or more beads between the bugle/seed on both sides. Three or 4 seed beads may also be used in place of bugle beads.

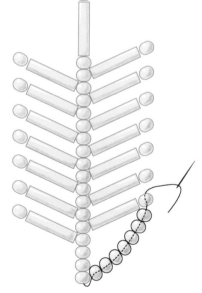

Figure 3

Palm Tree Frame
A palm tree made with six Palm Leaves
attached to a rope wrapped with seed beads is
glued to a picture frame.

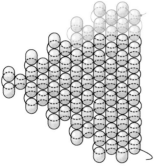

LEAF WITH JAGGED EDGE

Increasing and decreasing the edge with flat peyote stitch gives this triangular leaf its jagged edge, which with a little tuck, becomes three dimensional.

Materials

2 g size 11° seed beads

Thread a needle with ¾ yd (68.5 cm) of single thread.

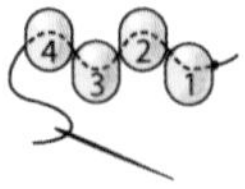

Figure 1

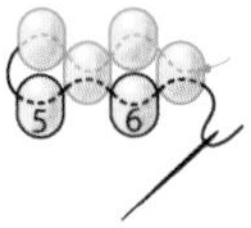

Row 1: Tie on 1 bead and add 3 more (Figure 1).

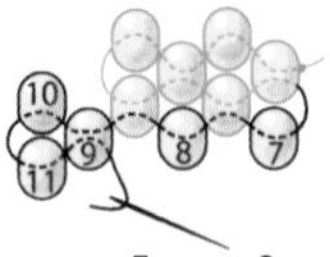

Row 2: Add 1 bead and go into the second bead from where the thread exited. Repeat this step once more (Figure 2).

Row 3: Turn and do peyote stitch across the row by adding a bead and going into the second bead in the previous row. At the end of the row add 3 beads. Go back through the first bead of the 3 just added (Figure 3). Continue to do peyote stitch across the row.

Figure 2

Continue to work back and forth with peyote stitch, increasing in the above manner on the same side until the leaf is the desired length; then decrease until there are 4 beads across to match the first row. To decrease, stop 1 peyote stitch before the end of the row, add 1 bead, turn and go back through the second bead from the end (Figure 4).

Figure 3

For a more dimensional leaf, make a little tuck along the bottom edge by bending the leaf slightly in half and stitching in place. Knot the thread and weave in the tail.

Figure 4

NETTED LEAF

Three-bead netting makes this
leaf quick and easy to do.

Figure 1

Figure 2

Materials

2 g size 11° seed beads

Figure 3

Thread a needle with ¾ yd (68 cm) of single thread and begin with the row
that forms the center of the leaf lengthwise.

Row 1: Tie on 1 seed bead leaving a 3–4" (8–10 cm) tail. This bead will be
left in the work. String on 17 more beads (for a larger leaf, begin with a
larger multiple of 4 beads plus 2). Go back through the next-to-last bead.

Row 2: *Add 3 beads. Go forward into the fourth bead counting from where
the thread exited a bead.* Repeat from * to * three more times so that the
thread is coming out of the tied-on bead (Figure 1).

Row 3: Without adding any beads, turn and go back through the last 2 beads
of the last set of 3, so that you are coming out of a middle or "point" bead.
Add 3 beads. Go into the middle bead of the next set of 3. Repeat from
* to * two more times (Figure 2).

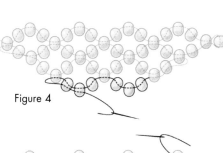

Figure 4

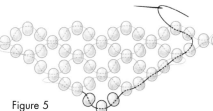

Figure 5

Continue going back and forth until there is only one set of 3 in the row
(Figures 3–5). Pass the thread along the beads on the edge and work the
other side of the leaf in the same manner (Figure 6). Knot the thread and
weave in the tail.

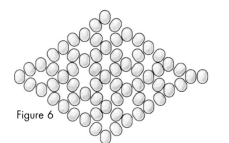

Figure 6

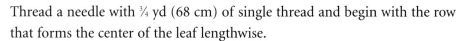

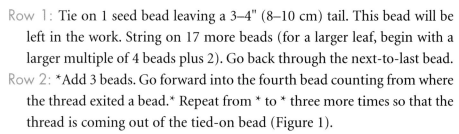

WATER LILY

This water lily is made of three sets of six petals graduated in size with an Easy Beaded Bead (see page 36) for the center. A creamy-colored bead, Delica #203, works well for the petals, but they may also be pale pink, such as Delica #071. After completing each petal, pass the thread through all the beads along the edge and pull tight to make the petal cup somewhat. Working with soft tension allows the petals to cup more easily.

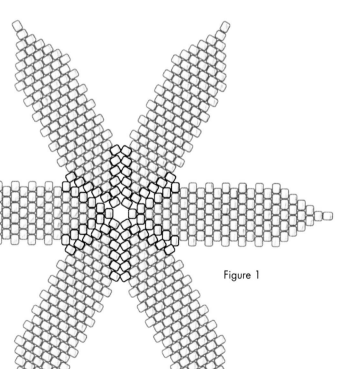

Back side of water lily

Materials

15 g cylinder beads

Following the instructions for the Oval Petals or Leaves on page 22, make the lily petals in the following sizes.

Six petals with 24-bead spines and 7 beads sticking up on each side

Six petals with 30-bead spines and 8 beads sticking up on each side

Six petals with 36-bead spines and 10 beads sticking up on each side

Join each group of six petals along the edge by square stitching (see page 108) the beads with a bold outline as shown in Figure 1; then align the centers of the large and medium petal sets and join at the center. Add the small set and sew it to the top of the first two. In the center add an Easy Beaded Bead (see page 36) made with pale green or yellow beads.

Figure 1

EASY BEADED BEAD

For this flower center, seed beads are wrapped around a base bead and the thread is passed through the hole of the base bead. For every other row, the first and last beads are shared with the previous row to create wedge-like shapes. You may wish to paint the base bead with nail polish to match the outside beads.

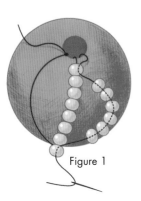

Materials

Base bead: ½" (12–14mm) round wood or plastic bead

3 g size 11° seed beads

Thread a needle with 1 yd (91.5 cm) of well-waxed single thread. Pass the thread through the hole of the base bead and tie the working thread tightly to the tail. Pass the thread through the base bead so it is exiting the top of the hole.

Add 8 seed beads (more or less depending on the size of the large bead and the seed beads) and go through the base bead again from bottom to top (Figure 1). Go through the first bead of the previous strand. Add 6 seed beads (or 2 less beads than the previous strand). Go through the last bead of the previous row, then through the base bead. Repeat from * to * seven more times. Knot the thread and weave in the tails.

Note: The hardest part of making this bead is keeping the seed beads from slipping into the hole of the base bead. To prevent slipping, hold your thumb on the bottom of the base bead and your forefinger on the top, moving your fingers slightly out of the way as the needle comes through.

Figure 1

STAR FLOWER WITH CURVED PETAL TIPS

Depending on the beads used, this lily-shaped flower may be made cupped or flat.

Materials

For a cupped flower: 10 g size 10° Miyuki triangle beads
For a flat flower: 10 g size 11° seed beads or cylinder beads

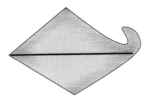

First we'll make the lower half of the petal, then the upper half.

Lower Half of Petal

Step 1. Thread a needle with 2 yd (183 cm) of thread and wax well. Add 1 bead and tie on the end of the thread leaving a 3–4" (8–10 cm) tail. This bead will be part of the work (Figure 1).

Figure 1

Step 2. Add 17 more beads for a total of 18 (Figure 2).

Figure 2

Step 3. Go back through the next-to-last bead (Figure 3).

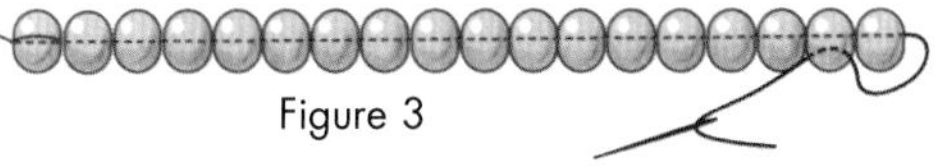

Figure 3

Step 4. Work peyote stitch back across the strand (pick up a bead, skip a bead, and go into the next bead); end by going into the first tied-on bead (Figure 4).

Figure 4

Step 5. Turn and, without adding a bead, go into the last bead added (edge decrease) (Figure 5).

Step 6. Continue in peyote stitch, decreasing at the beginning and end of each row (as in Step 5), until there is one bead on the final row.

Figure 5

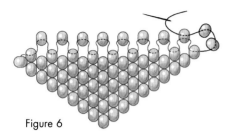

Figure 6

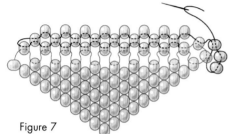

Figure 7

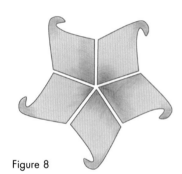

Figure 8

Upper Half of Petal

Step 7. Pass the thread through the beads so it is exiting the second bead from the beginning of the work and pointing toward the outer tip (Figure 6). Work peyote stitch across the row. After exiting the last bead in the row (the tip bead), add 2 beads and go back through the bead added just before the 2. The 2 new beads are shown in bold outline in Figure 6. These beads begin to form the curl at the outer end of the petal.

Step 8. Work back across the row. On the next row, decrease at the beginning edge as you did for the lower half of the petal in Step 5. When you come to the point where the 2 beads were added in the previous row, go through the first of the 2 beads, add 1 bead, then go through the second of the 2 beads. Now add 2 beads and go back through the bead squeezed in between the 2 beads. Work back across the row. Do a total of eight rows on this side of the petal (Figure 7), increasing on the tip end and decreasing on the stem end. Make five petals.

Joining the Petals

Step 9. Place two petals next to each other with the curls pointing in the same or different directions as shown in Figure 8; join (see Joining the Edges with Square Stitch on page 108). For the stamen, sew a bead, a button, or a cluster of beads in the center, or add the Stamen as shown on page 16.

Note: Seed beads and cylinder beads will make a flat flower. To make the flower cup with these beads, overlap the petals as you sew them together. Other beads such as hex beads, two-cuts, short bugles, or other more elongated beads may result in a more cup-shaped flower.

Two layers of
Star Flowers joined

MULTIPETAL FLOWER

Materials

5 g size 11° seed beads

6 or 8mm round bead

MULTIPETAL FLOWER WITH ROUND PETALS

Step 1. Thread a needle with 2 yd (183 cm) of thread, bring ends together, knot, clip the tails and melt the knot. String on 6 seed beads or the number needed to go halfway around the round bead. Pass the needle through the round bead so that the knot is near the bead. Separating the strands between the large round bead and the knot, pass the needle between the strands and pull tight (see Figure 1). This is the beginning of a lark's head knot.

Step 2. Add 6 seed beads or the number needed to go halfway around the round bead. Pass the needle through the round bead from the other end so that seed beads entirely encircle the round bead (Figure 2).

Step 3. Knot the thread and go through the first bead near the knot (Figure 3).

Step 4. Add 12 seed beads and go forward through the same seed bead in the ring again (in the same direction as the last pass), and through the next seed bead on the ring (Figure 4).

Step 5. Repeat Step 4 for each seed bead around the round bead. Knot the thread and weave in the tail.

MULTIPETAL FLOWER WITH POINTED PETALS

Work as above, except for each petal pick up 9 seed beads and go back through the next-to-last bead. Add 7 seed beads. Go forward through the same seed bead in the ring again and then through the next seed bead in the ring (Figure 5). Repeat this step around the bead. Petals will overlap.

This flower is worked around a large, round bead and may be made with round or pointed petals. The round bead can then be strung or sewn into other beadwork.

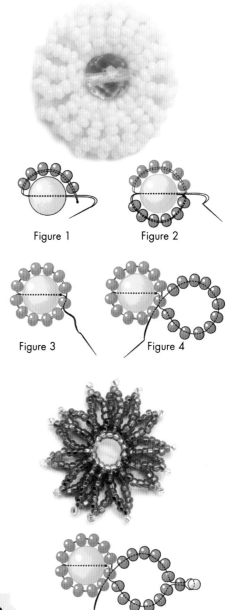

Figure 1

Figure 2

Figure 3

Figure 4

Figure 5

ROLLED FLOWERS

Inspiration for beaded flowers can come from many sources. For these flowers we take our cue from silk ribbon flowers, rolling a strip of beadwork and stitching it together as it is rolled. A strip of beads made by netting or peyote stitch with various types of fringes along one edge can be rolled and stitched. The strip may also be gathered before rolling. The way the strip is sewn together will determine the shape of the flower.

ROLLED FLOWER WITH LOOPS

Materials
5 g size 11° seed beads or cylinder beads

Step 1. Thread a needle with 1½ yd (137 cm) of single thread and tie 1 seed bead to the end, leaving a 3–4" (8–10 cm) tail. This bead will remain in the work. Add 13 more beads. Go back through the eleventh bead up the string (the fourth bead strung from the beginning, counting the tied-on bead). See Figure 1.

Step 2. Add 1 bead. Go through 2 beads (including the tied-on bead). Knot the working thread to the tail (Figure 2).

Step 3. Add 2 beads. Go through the bead to the right as shown in Figure 3.

Step 4. Pick up 11 beads. Go back through the first bead of the 11. Add 1 bead and go through the 2 beads to the left.

Continue until the work is 4–5" (10–13 cm) long. You may wish to make half the loops in a darker or lighter color.

Roll the beadwork and stitch together as shown on page 42.

Figure 1

Figure 2

Figure 3

ROLLED FLOWER WITH POINTED PETALS

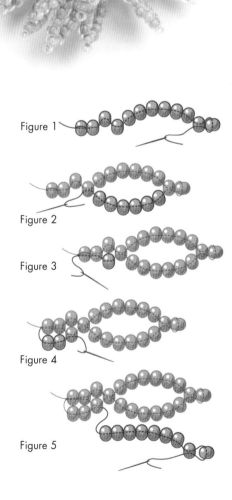

Materials

About 5 g size 11° seed beads or cylinder beads with contrasting beads for the tips if desired

Step 1. Thread a needle with 1½ yd (137 cm) of single thread and tie 1 seed bead to the end, leaving a 3–4" (8–10 cm) tail. This bead will remain in the work. Add 11 beads (10 plus 1 contrasting tip bead). Go back through the next-to-last bead (Figure 1).

Step 2. Add 6 beads. Go into the seventh bead on the previous string counting from where the thread exits a bead (Figure 2).

Step 3. Add 1 bead. Go through the next 2 beads (Figure 3).

Step 4. Add 2 beads, turn and go through the next bead (Figure 4).

Step 5. Add 9 beads (8 plus 1 contrasting tip bead) and go back through the next-to-last bead (Figure 5).

Repeat Steps 2–5 until the strip is 4" (10 cm) long.

To form the flower, roll the strip of beadwork and stitch together as shown on page 42.

Figure 1

Figure 2

Figure 3

Figure 4

Figure 5

Sewing the Rolled Flowers Together

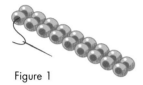

Figure 1

The way these flowers are assembled is important to their final appearance. Use this method for your first flower, but try other methods of your own.

Note: In order to simplify the illustrations, only the 2 bottom beads in the strip are shown.

Figure 2

Step 1. With 18" (45.5 cm) of single thread, exit the first 2 beads at the bottom of the strip (Figure 1) and join the first pair of beads to the fourth pair of beads by going up through the fourth pair and down through the first pair (Figure 2).

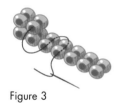

Figure 3

Step 2. Pass the needle up through the next pair of beads (the fifth pair) and down through the next pair (Figure 3).

Step 3. Roll the strip slightly. Pass the needle up through the pair of beads on the inner part of the roll that is closest to where the thread exited a pair of beads (Figure 4). Then go down through the same pair of beads in the outer part of the roll. Repeat this step to the end of the strip.

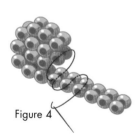

Figure 4

"If I had but two loaves of bread, I would sell one and buy hyacinths, for they would feed my soul."
—*The Koran*

Rolled Flower Pin

POM-POM FLOWER

This fantasy flower is made with a strip of lace chain that is gathered, rolled, and stitched.

Materials

12 g size 11° seed beads

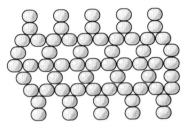

Lace Chain

Step 1. Thread a needle with 1½ yd (137 cm) of single thread and tie 1 seed bead to the end, leaving a 3–4" (8–10 cm) tail (Figure 1). This bead will remain in the work.

Step 2. Add 5 more beads and go back through the next-to-last bead (Figure 2).

Step 3. Add 3 beads and go into the first bead on the string—the tied-on bead (Figure 3).

Step 4. Add 3 beads and go back through the next-to-last bead (Figure 4).

Step 5. Add 3 beads and go into the middle bead of the last scallop of 3 beads just made (Figure 5).

Figure 1

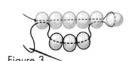

Figure 2

Figure 3

Figure 4

Figure 5

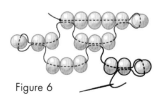
Figure 6

Step 6. Add 3 beads and go back through the next-to-last bead (Figure 6).

Step 7. Add 3 beads and go into the middle bead of the last scallop of beads (Figure 7).

Step 8. Repeat Steps 4 through 7 until the chain has 36 picots on each side. End by adding 1 set of 3 beads after the last picot and going into the middle bead of the next scallop.

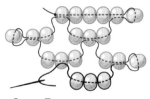
Figure 7

Knot the thread between the beads and pass the needle through to the tip bead on the opposite side. Now go through all the tip beads on this side. At the end of the strip, pull the thread so the beads are gathered together and touching. Knot the thread to hold the gather in place. This will be the bottom of the pom-pom.

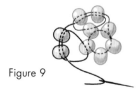
Figure 8

Form a ring with the last 5 picot beads by going forward through these 5 again. Roll the gather around the 5-bead ring. Stitch the picot beads from the outer roll to the inner roll with square stitch. For every single bead on the inner roll, go through 2 (or sometimes 3) beads on the outer roll (Figures 8 and 9). Continue until you reach the end of the strip, keeping the bottom of the roll flat.

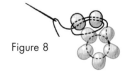
Figure 9

Figures 8 and 9 show the ring of 5 beads formed on the bottom of the flower with the beads sewn together with square stitch.

"God gave us memories so that we might have roses in December."
—J. M. Barrie

Escape from a Minnesota Winter
Rolled Flowers with Pointed Petals, Palm Leaves, small shells, pressed glass flowers, and branching fringe are sewn to a bib made of peyote stitch in variegated blues, which resemble water.

Collage Necklace IV
A flower made with six Oval Petals or Leaves is attached to random netting with beads and fringe accents.

SCOTTISH THISTLE

Netted bead

Make a Netted Bead (see below) in muted light green, then attach a Rolled Flower with Pointed Petals (see page 41). Thanks to Jane Langenback for combining the elements for this beautiful flower.

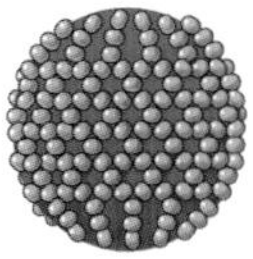

Materials for Base

14mm wood bead, colored green with permanent marker or nail polish

4 g size 11° seed beads, matte medium green

Materials for Stem

18-gauge wrapped stem wire

Materials for Petals

6 g cylinder beads for petals (suggested color: Delica #783)

2 g cylinder beads for tips (suggested color: Delica #694)

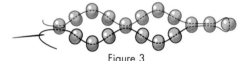

Figure 1

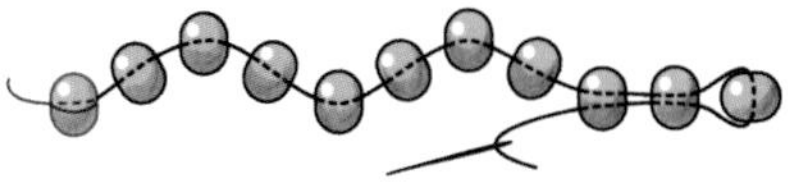

Figure 2

Figure 3

Netted Bead

Following the instructions below, make a strip of netting with picots on both sides long enough to go around the equator of the bead and then join the ends, gather the bottom edge, slip in the wood bead, and gather the top edge. Knot the thread and weave in the tails.

Step 1. Thread a needle with 1½ yd (137 cm) of single thread and tie 1 seed bead to the end, leaving a 3–4" (8–10 cm) tail (Figure 1). This bead will be left in the work.

Step 2. Add 10 more beads. Skip the last bead and go through two beads (Figure 2). (These 3 beads form a picot.)

Step 3. Add 3 beads. Go into the fourth bead in the previous row counting from where the thread exited a bead (scallop made). Repeat this step once. The thread should now be exiting the tied-on bead (Figure 3).

47

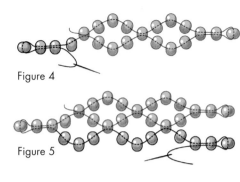
Figure 4

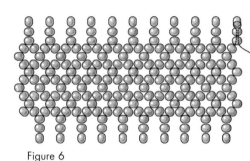
Figure 5

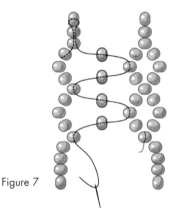
Figure 6

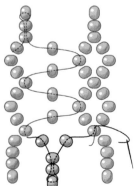
Figure 7

Figure 8

Step 4. Add 4 beads. Skip the last bead and go through two beads (picot made) (Figure 4).

Step 5. Add 3 beads. Go into the middle bead of the next 3-bead scallop in the previous row. Repeat this step once. Add 4 beads. Skip the last bead and go through two beads (Figure 5).

Step 6. Repeat Steps 3, 4, and 5 until there are 11 picots on one side and 10 on the other side and you have just come out of a picot. You will now be on the side opposite the tied-on bead (Figure 6).

Step 7. To lace up the sides to form a tube, hold the ending edge and the beginning edge so they are almost next to each other. Pick up 1 bead. Go into the middle bead of the scallop on the opposite side. Repeat three more times. The new beads are shown with a bold outline (Figure 7).

Step 8. Add 4 beads. Skip the last bead and go through two beads. Add 1 bead. Go into the tied-on bead. Knot the thread between the beads (Figure 8).

Step 9. Pass the thread through the work to the opposite side so that the thread is exiting a bead on the tip of the picot. Pass the thread through all the tip beads on that side. Pull the thread tight so that the tip beads are touching and the piece forms a cup. Go through all the tip beads again. Knot the thread.

Step 10. Pass the thread to the other side of the work and go through all the tip beads. Place the 14mm bead in the cup just formed, aligning the hole with the hole in the bottom of the cup. Pull the thread tight to close the cup. Go through all the tip beads again. Knot the thread and weave in the tails.

Step 11. Make a Rolled Flower with Pointed Petals according to the directions on page 41. Sew the flower to the Netted Bead.

Attaching Stem Wire to the Netted Bead

Apply white glue to the end of the stem wire that will be inserted into the netted bead. Wrap the end with sewing thread until it fits snugly inside the bead. Remove the wrapped end, apply white glue, and insert in the bead again. Allow the glue to dry.

To make a smaller Scottish Thistle, use a 10mm wood bead and size 14° seed beads. For the petals, make the petals 2 beads shorter and only 3½" (9 cm) long.

Leaves

Materials

5 g cylinder beads

Thread a needle with 1½ yd (137 cm) of thread, bring the ends together and wax well. Put 1 cylinder bead on the end of the thread and knot securely. Clip the tail close to the knot. Dab with clear nail polish. Add 2½" (6.5 cm) of cylinder beads. Skipping the last bead, work peyote stitch back down the stem, making short branches every 6 beads.

"And the heart that is soonest awake to the flowers is always the first to be touch'd by the thorns."
—*Thomas Moore*

Thistle Brooch on a Buckle Base
Three Scottish Thistles are wired to a buckle with branching fringe accents.

A life-size daffodil, a sure sign of spring! The daffodil is made in two parts: The upper cup-shaped petal is made with herringbone stitch similar to the Tiny Tulips on page 73 and the six petals are made with brick stitch.

Materials

20 g size 11° seed beads

Upper Cup-Shaped Petal

Row 1: Thread a needle with 2 yd (183 cm) single thread, add 10 beads and tie to form a ring.

Row 2: Add 4 beads and go into the next bead on the ring. Repeat nine more times. Go through the first 2 beads of the first set of 4 added (this is the jump up into position for the next row).

Row 3: Add 2 beads and go into the next bead of the set of 4 (these beads form the herringbone column), then into the second bead of the next set of 4 beads (Figure 1). Repeat nine more times. Go through the corner bead and the one above it to complete the row and the jump up to begin the next row (Figure 2).

Rows 4–11: Add 2 beads and go into the next bead of this herringbone column. Add 1 bead and go through the corner bead of the next herringbone column. Repeat nine more times. Go through the corner bead and the one above it to complete the row; jump up to begin the next row.

Row 12: Work as for Rows 4–11 but add 2 beads between the herringbone columns instead of 1.

Row 13: Add 3 beads and go into the next bead of this herringbone column. Add 3 beads and go through the corner bead of the next herringbone column. Repeat nine more times. Go through the corner bead and the one above it to complete the row. Knot the thread twice and weave in the tails.

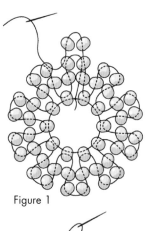

Figure 1

Figure 2

Lower Petals

The lower petals are made of six diamonds of brick stitch with elongated sides (Figure 3). (See Brick Stitch Basics on page 104.)

Thread a needle with 1½ yd (137 cm) of single thread. Make a base row 2 beads tall and 10 beads long. Beginning at the widest part of the petal and working toward the inner point, work 1-bead tall brick-stitch rows as follows: Decrease at the beginning and end of each of the following rows, locking the stitch at the beginning of each row.

Row 1: 8 beads across.
Row 2: 7 beads across.
Row 3: 6 beads across.
Row 4: 5 beads across.
Row 5: 4 beads across.
Row 6: 3 beads across.
Row 7: 2 beads across; add the single bead for Row 8 as you lock the stitch.

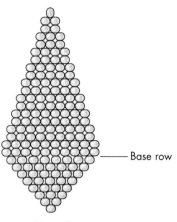

Base row

Figure 3

For the outer part of the petal, pass the thread up so it is exiting the first bead of the base row. Continue with 2-bead tall brick-stitch rows.

Rows 1–9: Add 4 beads, catch the second loop, lock the stitch (beginning edge decrease), work across the row but do not increase in the last loop (ending edge decrease). On Row 9, with only two stacks, add 1 tip bead as you lock in the stitch.

Join the six petals with square stitch along the sides of the inner part of the petal (see page 108). Sew the trumpet shape to the six petals by stitching from inside the cup through to the petals, then through a bead in the petals and back up to the inside of the cup. Add the stamen (see page 16). Add a stem (see page 12).

CALLA LILY

This flower is made by combining one of the Oval Petals or Leaves (page 22) with a Bulbous Stamen (page 17).

Materials

5 g cylinder beads

Make a peyote-stitch petal with a spine about 3" (7.5 cm) (about 51 spine beads) long and with the stem end flat instead of pointed (see Oval Petals or Leaves, Variation Five). To make the stem end flat, do not decrease on this end for three rows on each side. Continue with the decreases until there are about 8 sticking-up beads (Figure 1).

Wrap the petal around a Bulbous Stamen and sew to the beads along the bottom row.

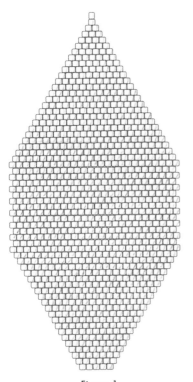

Figure 1

CLUSTER FLOWER

Cluster flowers such as lilacs can be made with a Bulbous Stamen (page 17) embellished with tiny flower beads, 4mm bicone crystals, or a size 6° or a size 8° bead topped with a size 11° or 14°. For example, after completing a stamen of desired size, exit a bead in the stamen, then add a size 6° and size 11° seed bead. Go back through the size 6° and then into the next bead in the stamen. Add beads around the stamen row by row (Figure 1). After adding the embellishment, pass the thread through the bead marked 1. Then add more embellishment beads and go through the bead marked 2, and continue spiraling up the stamen.

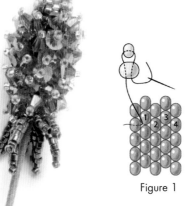

Figure 1

Row 11: Pass the thread down through the beads so that you are exiting the top of the first stack of Row 6 (see arrow in Figure 1a). Pick up 1 bead. Pass needle between the 2 beads in the end stack of Row 7 and back through the new bead. (This bead and the next 4 will sit perpendicular to the beads they are attached to.) Work four more stitches like this along the edge. The next two single-bead stitches are worked in the first loop after turning the corner. Work seven 2-bead stitches (increase once in the middle loop). Work two 1-bead stitches in the last loop along the top and five more down the other side, connecting between beads as you did on the first side. Pass the thread through the last stack of beads in Row 6. Knot the thread and weave in the tails.

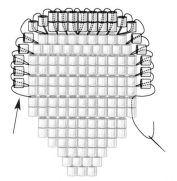

Figure 1a shows how Row 11 is added.

Front Petal

Thread a needle with 1½ yd (137 cm) single thread and work the petal as described below. The letters in parentheses at the end of the row indicate the order in which the beads are picked up. Note the number of beads in each stack and where the increases and decreases occur. Be sure to lock the stitch on the rows with decreases at the beginning edge.

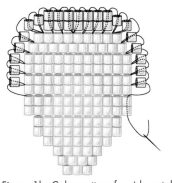

Figure 1b: Color pattern for side petals.

Row 1 (base row): 1-bead stacks, 3 stacks across. (A, A, A, A)
Row 2: 1-bead stacks, increase beginning and end—4 stacks across. (B, A, A, B)
Row 3: 1-bead stacks, increase beginning, middle, and end—6 stacks across. (B, B, B, B, B, B)
Row 4: 2-bead stacks, increase beginning, middle, and end—8 stacks across. (BA, BB six times, AB)
Row 5: 2-bead stacks, increase beginning, third, fifth, and end loops—11 stacks across. (AA, BB nine times, AA)
Row 6: 2-bead stacks, increase beginning, third, fifth, seventh, and end loops—15 stacks across. (AA twice, AB twice, BB three times, AB, BB three times, AB twice, AA twice)
Row 7: 2-bead stacks, increase beginning, third, fifth, seventh, tenth, twelfth,

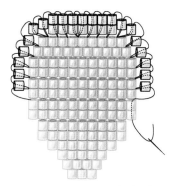

Figure 1c: Color pattern for back petals.

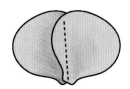

Figure 2

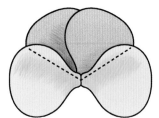

Figure 3

Figure 4

Figure 5

and last loops—21 stacks across. (AA seven times, AB twice, AA three times, AB twice, AA seven times)

Row 8: 1-bead stacks, decrease beginning, increase twice evenly spaced in row—22 stacks across. (Work A across row)

Row 9: The first two stacks are 1 bead tall with a beginning edge decrease (catch the second loop). All remaining stacks except the last two are 2 beads tall. Increase third, fifth, eighth, fourteenth, seventeenth, and nineteenth loops—24 stacks across. (Work Color A as follows: two 1-bead stacks, 2-bead stack with size 14° and cylinder, 2-bead stack nine times, 1-bead stack, 2-bead stacks nine times, 2-bead stack with size 14° and cylinder, 1-bead stack twice.)

Sew petals together and add 2 fringe beads in the center to form a pansy as shown. See Joining Edges with Square Stitch on page 108.

Joining the Petals

Step 1. Sew the two back petals together, overlapping slightly (Figure 2).

Step 2. Sew side petals to back petals as shown (Figure 3).

Step 3. Sew front petal to back and side petals. Add drop beads at the center (Figure 4).

Step 4. Optional: With black thread, embroider lines as shown on top of the pansy petals (Figure 5). If desired, sew a wrapped stem wire to the back of the pansy.

A flower made with five of the upper pansy petals overlapped and sewn together.

MORNING GLORY

This morning glory is a trumpet-shaped flower made with brick stitch using cylinder beads in colors that blend from deeper in the center to lighter on the outer edge. It is made flat with brick stitch and square stitch; joining the edges creates the trumpet shape.

Materials

   3 g each cylinder beads in three to five colors

   2 g size 11° or 14° seed beads for edge

   2 g cylinder beads in green for stems

For the flower, cylinder beads are used throughout except on the final row, which uses seed beads in size 11° or 14°. All brick-stitch stacks are 2 beads tall. The flower will be eleven rows of brick stitch with one additional row of seed beads on the edge. Work with soft tension. Always increase in the last loop every row (put two stacks in one loop).

Thread a needle with 1½ yd (137 cm) of single thread.

Row 1: Leaving an 18" (45.5 cm) tail that will be used later to make a stem, make a base row 2 beads tall and four stacks long using green cylinder beads (see Brick Stitch Basics on page 104).

Figure 1

Row 2: Turn the work so that you are working left to right; continue with green beads. Add 4 beads. Catch the first loop and go back up through the last 2 beads added (Figure 1). Add 2 beads, catch the middle loop and go back up through the last 2 beads (Figure 2). Add 2 beads, catch the next loop and go

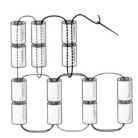

Figure 2

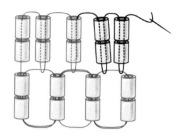

Figure 3

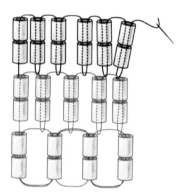

Figure 4

new color

previous color

Figure 5

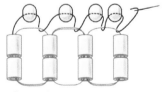

Figure 6

back up through the last 2 beads. Increase by adding 2 beads, catching the same loop again, and going back up (Figure 3). Row 2 is now complete—five stacks across the row.

Row 3: Continue with green beads. Add 4 beads, catch the first loop and go back up. Put one stack above each of the next two loops, and two stacks in the last loop (Ending edge increase, Figure 4). Row 3 complete—six stacks across the row.

Row 4: Begin color blending from green to Color A (deepest). The color pattern is shown in Figure 5. Add beads as follows:

First 4 beads: #1 and #2 are green, #3 is A; #4 is green. Catch first loop and go back up through last 2 beads.

Add beads #5 and #6 in A, catch next loop and go back up.

Add #7, A and #8, green. Catch next loop and go back up.

Increase: Add #9 and #10 in green, catch the same loop again and go back up.

Add #11 in A and #12 in green, catch the next loop and go back up.

Add beads #13 and #14 in A, catch next loop and go back up.

Increase: Add #15, A and #16, green. Catch the same loop and go back up.

    Row 4 complete—eight stacks across the row.

Row 5: Increase in every other loop across the row using only Color A—eleven stacks.

Row 6: Continue to increase in every other loop; transition from Color A to Color B following the pattern in Figure 5. Repeat the pattern from 5 and 6 to 11 and 12. (*Note:* always put two stacks in the last loop even though it breaks the pattern.) Row 6 complete—sixteen stacks across the row.

Row 7: Continue to increase in every other loop across the row using only Color B—twenty-three stacks.

Row 8: Increase across the row in every other loop and transition from Color B to Color C—thirty-four stacks.

Row 9: Increase in every other loop across the row using only Color C—fifty stacks.

Row 10: Increase across the row in every other loop and transition from Color C to Color D—seventy-four stacks.

Row 11: Increase in every other loop across the row using only Flower Color D—one hundred and ten stacks.

Row 12: Add edge beads that lie on their sides and cover the thread loops. Use size 11° or 14° seed beads in light color. Pick up 1 bead, catch first loop (do not go back up through the bead). Pick up 1 bead and catch the next loop. Continue across the row (Figure 6). Put 2 beads in the last loop, one at a time. Knot between the beads and leave the tail to join the sides.

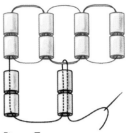

Figure 7

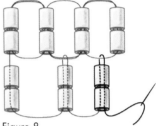

Figure 8

The Rows at a Glance
Check them off as you work

Row	Color	Stks	Loops
1	G	4	3
2	G	5	4
3	G	6	5
4	G>A	8	7
5	A	11	10
6	A>B	16	15
7	B	23	22
8	B>C	34	33
9	C	50	49
10	C>D	74	73
11	D	110	109

Making the Flower Stem

Thread a needle with the 18" (45.5 cm) tail left from the start of the flower.

Row 1: Add 4 beads and, skipping the first loop, catch the thread between the two middle stacks of beads (decrease). Go back through the last 2 beads (Figure 7).

Add 2 beads and catch the thread between the third and fourth stacks (Figure 8). You have now decreased from four stacks to three stacks.

Row 2: Turn the work. Add 4 beads and, skipping the first loop, catch the thread between the second and third stacks of beads (decrease). Go back through the last 2 beads (Figure 9).

Row 3: Add 2 beads, go up through 2 beads in the column next to where the thread exited, cross over and go down through 2 beads next to it, then down through 1 bead in the new row (square stitch, Figure 10).

Continue this step until the stem is the desired length, usually about twelve rows of square stitch. Knot the thread and weave in the tail.

Finishing: Sew the sides of the flower together with square stitch from the top edge to the row with three stacks. (See Joining Edges with Square Stitch, page 108.)

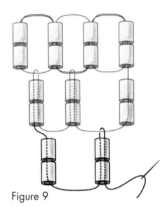

Figure 9

Figure 10

This exotic bloom is native to Brazil and grows in a wide variety of color patterns. For a lovely Cattleya orchid, you will need to make three types of petals: three narrow oval petals with brick stitch; two peyote-stitch oval petals with ruffled edges; and one cone-shaped brick-stitch center front petal with a ruffled edge.

Materials

5 g each cylinder beads, colors A and B*

4 g each size 11° seed beads colors A and B (A and B colors should match the cylinder bead colors)*

6mm pearl

*In the diagrams, A beads are shown in purple and B beads are shown in pink.

Narrow Petals (Make 3)

Thread a needle with 1½ yd (137 cm) single thread. Using cylinder beads in colors A and B, follow the color pattern in Figure 1, leaving an 18" (45.5 cm) tail at the beginning of the row. Begin with the middle row of eight stacks 3 beads tall and work first one side, decreasing at the beginning and end of each row (locking the stitch at the beginning of each row) until you have a row of two stacks. Add one bead as you lock in this row. Knot the thread and weave in the tail. (See Brick Stitch Basics, page 104.)

For the remaining half, thread the tail in the needle. Work each row 3 beads tall, decreasing at the beginning and end of each row until you are ready to begin the row that is four stacks across. Work the remaining rows with 1-bead stacks until you have 1 bead in the last row. Add this bead as you lock in the stitch in the previous row.

Ruffled Oval Petals (Make 2)

Thread a needle with 1 yd (91.5 cm) single thread. Following the directions for Variation Five of the Oval Petals or Leaves on page 24, make each petal 29 beads long. Use cylinder beads in Color B for the 29 beads and the first row of peyote stitch on one side. Complete this petal using seed beads in Color A and following the directions for the Ruffled Edge Leaf on page 24. Add a ruffle with seed beads in Color B.

Cone-Shaped Center Front Petal (Make 1)

Thread a needle with 2½ yd (229 cm) single thread and work this petal in brick stitch with cylinder beads in Color A, beginning at the outer point of the cone (the bottom of the graph). Note that Rows 3 and 6 have an extra bead at the beginning and end of each row (see Beginning Edge Extension and Ending Edge Extension below); Rows 17 and 18 have decreases in the middle of the row (Figure 2).

Row 1: 2-bead stacks—3 beads across.

Row 2: 1-bead stacks—4 beads across.

Row 3: 1-bead stacks, increase beginning* and end**—7 beads across.

Row 4: 1-bead stacks—8 beads across.

Row 5: 1-bead stacks—9 beads across.

Row 6: 2-bead stacks, increase beginning and end—12 beads across.

Row 7: 1-bead stacks—11 beads across.

Row 8: 1-bead stacks—12 beads across.

Row 9: 1-bead stacks—13 beads across.

Row 10: 2-bead stacks—14 beads across.

Row 11: 2-bead stacks—15 beads across.

Row 12: 2-bead stacks—14 beads across.

Row 13: 2-bead stacks—13 beads across.

Row 14: 2-bead stacks—12 beads across.

Row 15: 2-bead stacks—11 beads across.

Row 16: 2-bead stacks—10 beads across.

Row 17: 2-bead stacks, decrease mid-row—8 beads across.

Row 18: 2-bead stacks, decrease mid-row—6 beads across.

Row 19: 2-bead stacks—5 beads across.

*See Beginning Edge Extension below.

**See Ending Edge Extension on page 64.

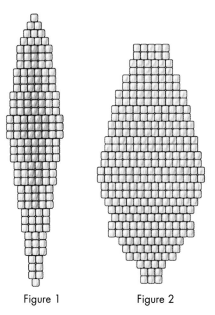

Figure 1   Figure 2

BEGINNING EDGE EXTENSION

Add two stacks of beads, pass the thread under the first thread bridge, and go back up the last stack (Figure 3).

Figure 3

Go down the first stack and then add a stack of beads (Figure 4).

Figure 4

Figure 5

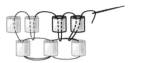

Figure 6

Figure 7

Go down through the second stack in the row and up through the third stack (Figure 5).

ENDING EDGE EXTENSION
Work two brick stitches, one at a time in the last loop. Thread should be exiting the top of the last bead (Figure 6).

Add one stack of beads. Catch the thread at the bottom of the previous stack and then go back up through the last stack (Figure 7).

SHAPING THE CONE
Join Rows 17, 18, and 19 with square stitch to form a tube (see Joining Edges with Square Stitch on page 108). Continuing with the same thread, and working with seed beads in Color B, add 3-bead loops around the front open edge so they form a ruffle (See Oval Petals or Leaves, Variation Four with ruffled edge on page 24.)

Assembly
Join the Narrow Petals to the Ruffled Oval Petals with square stitch where they naturally join, alternating the petals as shown in Figure 8. Do not include the ruffle in the joined edge.

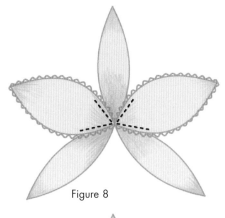

Figure 8

With the top of the petal at the center of the flower, sew the Cone-Shaped Center Petal to the top, stitching through and between beads until it is secure. To form the stamen: With thread exiting the cone center, add 7 cylinder beads, a 6mm pearl and 1 seed bead, then go back through the pearl and the cylinder beads. Bring thread to the wrong side, knot it, and weave in the tail (Figure 9).

Figure 9

Orchid Lei
(Collaboration of Bonnie Voelker and the author)
A Cattleya Orchid embellishes a collar crocheted with copper wire and dyed shell chips.

Rose Garden Hat
Roses and leaves attached
to a velvet hatband.

ROSE

This rose is made with a strip of flat peyote 10" (25cm) long and 6 beads wide with an extra bead every row on the top edge and an extra bead every other row on the bottom edge (see Figure 8 on page 68). The beads shown in white in the diagrams should be in a slightly darker or slightly lighter color, but they should be easily distinguishable from the other beads. For now, we'll call these beads "X." The main color beads will be referred to simply as "beads."

Materials

15 g main color size 11° seed beads, 2 g contrasting color

The new beads in each step are shown with a bold outline. Work with medium/soft tension.

Figure 1

Step 1. Thread a needle with 1½ yd (137 cm) of single thread. Tie 1 X bead on the end of the thread leaving a 3–4" (8–10 cm) tail (Figure 1). This bead will be left in the work.

Figure 2

Step 2. Add 5 more beads (Figure 2).

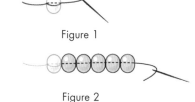

Figure 3

Step 3. Add 2 beads, turn and go back through the fourth bead counting from the needle end. Work two more peyote stitches across the row. (To do peyote stitch, add 1 bead, skip a bead, and go through 1 bead, Figure 3.) End exiting the tied-on bead.

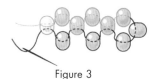

Figure 4

Step 4. Add 1 bead and 1 X bead, turn and go into the last bead added in the previous row, then work two more peyote stitches (Figure 4).

Step 5. Add 2 beads, turn and go into the last bead added in the previous row, then work two more peyote stitches (Figure 5).

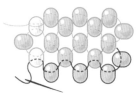

Figure 5

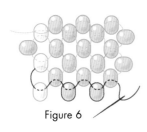

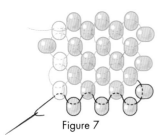

Figure 6

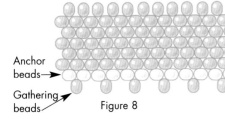

Figure 7

Top of strip

Anchor beads→

Gathering beads→

Figure 8

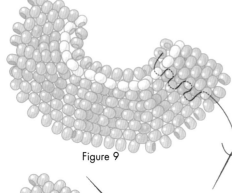

Figure 9

Figure 10

Step 6. Add 1 X bead, turn and go into the last bead added in the previous row, then work two more peyote stitches (Figure 6).

Step 7. Add 2 beads, turn and go into the last bead added in the previous row, then work two more peyote stitches (Figure 7).

Repeat the directions from Step 4 to Step 7 until the piece is 10" (25 cm) long. Knot the thread and weave in the tails. The piece should look like Figure 8.

Note: "Down" refers to pointing the needle toward the bottom of the rose and up toward the top, regardless of how you hold the strip.

Forming the Rose

Thread a needle with 1 yd (91.5 cm) of single thread and anchor it so it is coming out of the first extra bead along the bottom. The beads below the X beads will now be referred to as the "gathering beads" and the X beads will be referred to as the "anchor beads" (Figure 8). Go through all the gathering beads along the bottom edge toward the beginning. Pull tight so the piece gathers with no extra thread between the beads. Knot the thread between beads to secure the gather.

Lay the piece in front of you with the gathering beads away from you and the working thread on the right. To form the center of the rose, roll the right vertical edge to the left so it forms a tube about ⅜" (1 cm) in diameter. It is important to do it this way because it's much easier to sew the piece together. Weave the vertical edge beads to the strip to form the center tube and then run the thread back down toward the gathering beads. Go through 2 or 3 gathering beads (see Figures 9 and 10).

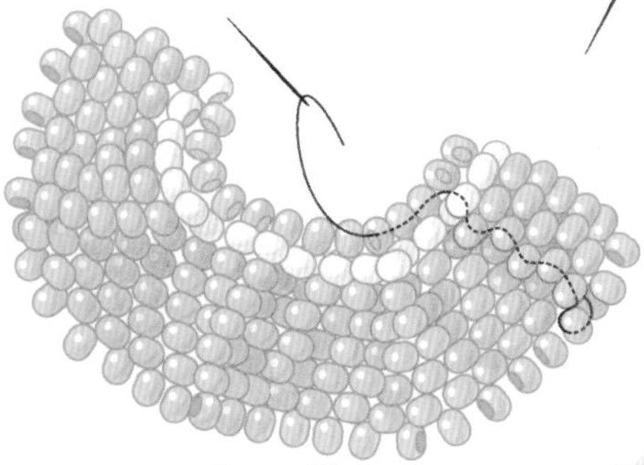

TINY TULIPS

Make a variety of flowers based on this herringbone pattern by increasing the number of beads in the beginning ring and then increasing the number of beads between the herringbone columns.

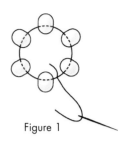

Figure 1

Materials

    100 cylinder beads
    1 green sequin, optional
    1 size 8° green seed bead
    36 size 11° green seed beads

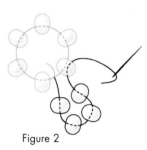

Figure 2

Row 1: Thread a needle with 1 yd (91.5 cm) of single thread, add 6 beads and tie into a ring (Figure 1).

Row 2: Add 4 beads and go into the next bead on the ring. Repeat this step five more times (Figure 2). Each set of 4 beads is the beginning of a herringbone column.

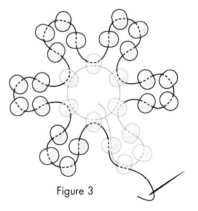

Figure 3

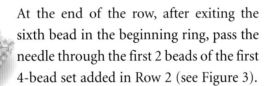

At the end of the row, after exiting the sixth bead in the beginning ring, pass the needle through the first 2 beads of the first 4-bead set added in Row 2 (see Figure 3).

Row 3: Continue with the herringbone stitch as follows: Add 2 beads and go down into the next bead (third bead) in the 4-bead set. Then go into the second bead of the next 4-bead set on the ring—the corner bead—going upward (Figure 4). Repeat these two steps five more times. At the end of the row, go through the next corner bead and the bead above it. (This is the jump up through 2 beads to begin the new row.)

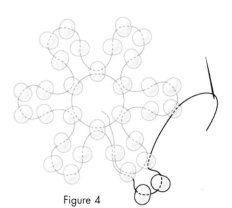

Figure 4

73

Rows 4–6: Add 2 beads for the herringbone column (up through the corner bead and down through the bead next to it), and then go into the corner bead of the next herringbone column. Repeat five more times. Hold the work so it begins to form a cup. Jump up at the end of the row.

Row 7: Follow directions for Row 3, but add 3 beads instead of 2 for the herringbone column and add 1 bead before going into the corner bead of the next herringbone column. Doing so makes the edge flare out slightly and makes points on the edge of the petals.

Stem

Cut 22-gauge stem wire 2.5" (6.5 cm) long. Put 1 bead on the end and secure it in place by bending the wire around it. Pass the wire through the hole in the bottom of the flower so the bead is inside. Add 1 green sequin or size 8° green seed bead. String on 2" (5 cm) of size 11° green seed beads. Bend a loop in the bottom of the wire to hold the beads on the wire.

A slightly larger tulip may be made with a beginning ring of 8 beads instead of 6 and working one more row before Row 7 where the points of the petals are added.

Tiny Tulip Earrings
Tiny Tulips and pressed glass leaves are attached to an earring finding with short strands of beads.

Tiny Tulips with Vase
Tiny Tulips and Long Thin Leaves are arranged in a brass vase.

Flower Box Picture Frame

A rectangle of wood is covered on the sides with brick stitch done with 4mm cube beads and on the top with a flat peyote-stitched strip in green. This unit is glued to a picture frame. Flowers are clusters of Tiny Tulips. Background grass is made with random lengths of Daisy petals. Leaves are made with the Tiny Daffodil base.

Many shapes and sizes of flowers can be made with the herringbone stitch, sometimes referred to as the Ndebele stitch. Flowers can be flat, slightly cupped, or worked around an oval or round bead. For all of them we'll begin the same way that the Tiny Tulip is begun—with a ring of beads, and on the second row with 4 beads between every 2 beads (see Figures 1–3 on page 73). In the Tiny Tulip, columns of beads are formed vertically as shown in Figure 4, page 73, but beads can be added between the columns to make them spread apart or flare out. These beads are added after going down through the second bead in the herringbone column as shown where the arrow points in Figure 1. Instructions are given for a slightly cupped flower and for one worked around a wood bead.

CUPPED FLOWER

Materials

3 g cylinder beads

Rows 1–3: Thread a needle with 1 yd (91.5 cm) of single thread and follow the directions for Rows 1–3 of the Tiny Tulip on page 73, except begin with 10 beads instead of 6.

Row 4: Add 2 beads to each herringbone column (up through the corner bead and down through the bead next to it), and add 1 bead (a connecting bead) before going into the corner bead of the next herringbone column. Jump up at the end of the row by going through the first bead added in the row (Figure 1).

Row 5: To make a point at the tip of a petal, add 3 beads instead of 2 and go down into the next bead of the herringbone column, then go through the connecting bead of the previous row again before going to the next herringbone column.

Figure 1

Sunflower Brooch
Cupped Herringbone Flowers with small black buttons for centers and artificial leaves are shown in a Brooch Flower Holder.

HERRINGBONE FLOWER WITH BASE BEAD

Materials

4 g cylinder beads
14mm wood base bead

Rows 1–3: Thread a needle with 1 yd (91.5 cm) of single thread and follow the directions for Rows 1–3 of the Tiny Tulip on page 73, except begin with 10 beads instead of 6.

Rows 4–11: Add 2 beads for the herringbone column (up through the corner bead and down through the bead next to it), and add 1 bead (connector bead) before going into the corner bead of the next herringbone column. Jump up at the end of each row.

Row 12: Insert the base bead in the tube that you've formed. Add 2 beads for the herringbone column (up through the corner bead and down through the bead next to it), but do not add the connector bead before going into the corner bead of the next herringbone column. Doing so cinches in the tube and holds the base bead in place. Be sure the hole of the base bead is aligned with the hole in the bottom of the tube.

Rows 13–15: In each row, increase the number of connector beads from one to three to make the edge flare out.

Row 16: To make the points on the end of each petal, add 3 beads instead of 2 and go into the corner bead of the herringbone column, then go through the 3 connecting beads of the previous row again before going to the next herringbone column. Knot the thread and weave in the tails.

For a stem, see page 12. Add a Flat Calyx if desired (see page 20, but begin with 7 beads instead of 5 and make seven points instead of five).

The Daffodils

I wandered lonely as a cloud
That floats on high o'er vales and hills,
When all at once I saw a crowd,
A host, of golden daffodils,
Beside the lake, beneath the trees,
Fluttering and dancing in the breeze.

Continuous as the stars that shine
And twinkle on the milky way,
They stretched in never-ending line
Along the margin of a bay:
Ten thousand saw I at a glance
Tossing their heads in sprightly dance.

The waves beside them danced, but they
Out-did the sparkling waves in glee:
A Poet could not be but gay
In such a jocund company!
I gazed—and gazed—but little thought
What wealth the show to me had brought:

For oft, when on my couch I lie
In vacant or in pensive mood,
They flash upon that inward eye
Which is the bliss of solitude;
And then my heart with pleasure fills,
And dances with the daffodils.

—William Wordsworth

(1770–1850)

Materials

2 g size 11° seed beads

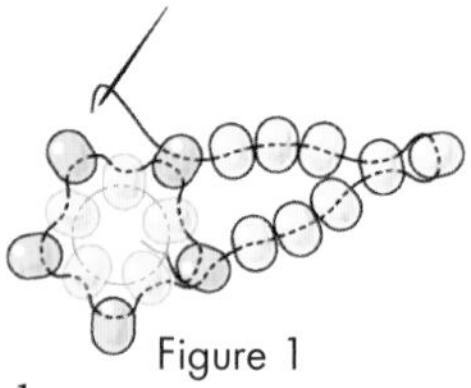

Begin with Rows 1 and 2 of the Lily of the Valley (see page 84), except use size 11° beads. On the next row, add the beads as shown in Figure 1, between each pair of beads that is sticking up as follows: Add 5 beads, go back through the next-to-last bead; add 3 beads and go into the next bead that is sticking up. The piece should now look like a flat star. Now pass the thread back to the second row of 5 beads and work five rows of even-count peyote stitch upward from the base (see page 106). For the sixth row, add 2 beads between every 2 beads instead of 1 to make the top edge flare out slightly.

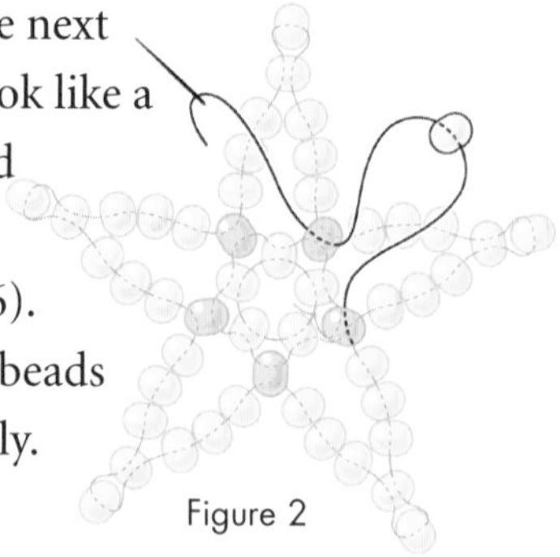

Figure 1

Figure 2

Stem

See Stem for Tiny Tulip on page 74.

A second method of adding the stem is to attach a size 8° bead to the end of a 3" (7.5 cm) piece of 22-gauge stem wire and hold it in place by bending the wire around it. Insert the wire into the flower so the bead is inside. Add a drop of white glue to the bottom of the flower and then add a sequin to the wire and push it to the bottom of the flower. Add another drop of white glue and wrap the stem wire with thread until the flower is held firmly in place. Add another drop of white glue to hold the tail in place.

Leaves

See Long Thin Leaves on page 28, or purchase artificial leaves and cut to fit.

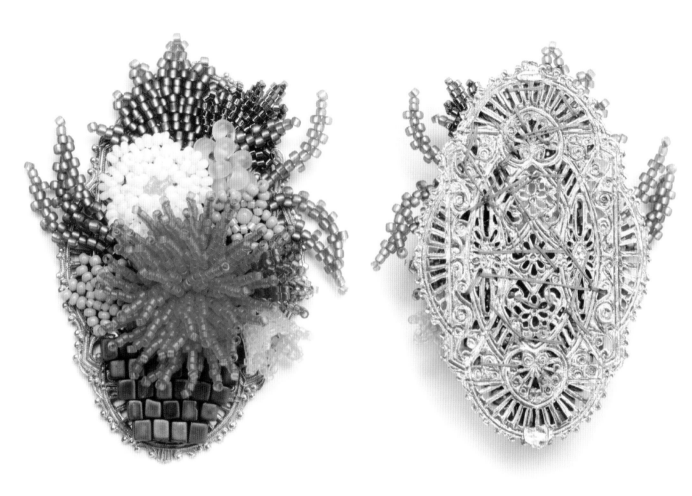

Flower Pot Brooch
Various small flowers and leaves are attached to a filigree metal plate with a small brick-stitch pot made with 4mm cube beads.

Back of brooch. Cover back of brooch with a second matching filigree plate and wire them together at the edge. Glue on a pin back.

These little lilies may also be used as bells, other flowers that have a bell-like shape, thimbles, tiny hats, or other cup-shaped items. For lilies of the valley, the shapes look best worked with size 14° beads in a cream color. Attach with a few seed beads to a stem.

Figure 1

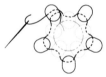

Figure 2

Figure 3

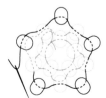

Figure 4

Materials

2 g size 14° seed beads

Row 1: Thread a needle with 1 yd (91.5 cm) of single thread, add 5 beads and tie to form a ring (Figure 1).

Row 2: Add 1 bead and go into the next bead. Repeat four more times (Figure 2). At the end of the row, go through the first bead added in this row (the jump up to start a new row, similar to even-count tubular peyote stitch, Figure 2.)

Rows 3–6: Add 1 bead and go into the next bead that is sticking up. Repeat four more times (Figure 3). At the end of each row, go through the first bead added in this row (Figure 4). Pinch the shape and keep the thread tight so that the work begins to form a cup.

Row 7: To make the top edge flare out, add 2 beads instead of 1 and go into the next bead that is sticking up. Repeat four more times. Knot the thread and weave in the tail. Add stem and leaves.

Stem and Leaves

Materials

3 g size 11° green seed beads
1 size 8° or 11° yellow bead

Thread a needle with 1 yd (91.5 cm) of thread, bring the ends together, and tie 1 green size 11° seed bead on the end of the thread. Knot securely and clip the tail close to the knot. Dab with clear nail polish. String on 2" (5cm) of beads, go through the lily from the bottom, add a yellow size 8° or 11° bead, go back through the lily, and work peyote stitch back down the stem, making short branches every 6 beads. Add more stems as you wish.

BROOCH FLOWER HOLDER

This tiny flower holder, shaped like a narrow funnel, is a great way to show off your tiny beaded flower collection.

Materials

3 g cylinder beads
3mm round bead or size 8° seed bead
Pin back, 1½" (3.8 cm) long
Flat-backed sew-ons or other beads for embellishing

Beginning at the bottom of the funnel with 1½ yd (137 cm) of single thread, make a base row of brick stitch 2 beads tall and six stacks of beads across (see Brick Stitch Base Row, page 104). Work in brick stitch for fifteen rows, increasing at the beginning and end of each row. Sew the pin back along the center of the piece. Join the long edges of the piece with square stitch to form a tube (see Joining Edges with Square Stitch, page 108). At the bottom, sew the 3mm round bead to fill the hole and make a decorative ending. Embellish the top edge as desired. Dip the funnel in Future Acrylic Floor Polish to stiffen it, being careful not to clog the closure on the pin back. Allow to dry.

> *"Let a hundred flowers blossom*
> *and a hundred schools of*
> *thought content."*
> *—Mao Tse-Tung*

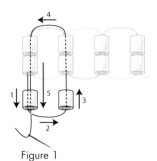

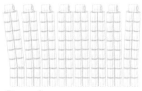

Figure 1

Figure 2

10-petal flower
variation

EIGHT-PETAL FLOWER

This eight-petal flower is made without a stem and may be used alone or attached to other flowers as a stamen.

Materials

3 g cylinder beads

8mm bead

Step 1. Thread the needle with 1½ yd (91.5 cm) of single thread in a color close to the beads. Following the instructions for Brick Stitch Base Row, make a strip 2 beads tall and sixteen stacks long (see Brick Stitch Basics, page 104).

Petals

Step 2. Add 2 beads. Go through the second stack of beads in the base row. Go back through the first stack and through the first of the 2 new beads (Figure 1). Continue to add 2 beads with square stitch by adding 2 beads, going back through 2 beads and forward through 3 beads until the petal is 8 beads tall, including the base-row beads.

Step 3. Add 1 bead and go through all the petal beads so that you are exiting a bead in the base row. Pass the thread through the next stack in the base row. Work seven more petals as described in Steps 2 and 3 (Figure 2).

Step 4. Join the base-row beads so that the petals form a ring. Sew the 8mm bead to the center of the flower by going through it and through 2 beads on the opposite side of the ring, then back through the 8mm and into 2 beads at the beginning of the base row. Knot the thread and weave in the tails.

Step 5. Dip the petals in Future Acrylic Floor Polish to stiffen. Spread them out and let them dry upside down.

DAISY

Materials

4 g white cylinder beads

1 size 18 (⅞₆") Dritz Half Ball Cover Button

1" (2.5 cm) square bright yellow cotton knit fabric

Follow the directions for the Eight-Petal Flower, except make the base row 1 bead tall and 24 beads long. Work twelve petals as described in Steps 2 and 3, then work a second set of petals on the same base beads, but place the petals between the previous petals. Cover the button with fabric according to the manufacturer's directions. Working from the underside of the daisy, overcast the petals to the edge of the button along the side edge, catching only the thread loop at the bottom of the base row so that the petals extend outward from the side of the button as daisy petals do. Join the petal strip and work one petal to complete the flower.

Materials

   4 g cylinder beads

   1 size 18 (⁷⁄₁₆") Dritz Half Ball Cover Button

   1" (2.3 cm) square yellow or lime green cotton knit fabric

Follow the directions for the Daisy Base Row (page 87).

Petals

Exiting the base row, add 8 beads and go back through the first 7 beads and into the base-row bead again. Go into the next base-row bead and add another petal. Continue to add petals across the base row. Add a second layer of petals to the same base beads. Sew to the button base as for the Daisy.

Gift Bag
A three-layer Daisy and Netted Leaves are attached to a small gift bag.

Book Cover with Poppies, Daisies, and Fleabane
An album with a recessed area in the cover is embellished
with Daisies, a Poppy, Fleabane and leaves made with brick
stitch and branching fringe.

BEETLE

Quick and easy to make, this beetle can sit on a leaf; glued to a tie-tack pin back, he can grace a collar; or with earring findings, he can crawl on your ear.

Materials

Flat pendant-type bead with hole at the top
about 14x25mm
2 g size 14° seed beads
2 size 8° black seed beads for eyes
2 size 11° seed beads in bright color (optional)
527 Glue or E-6000 Glue

Make two wings following the instructions for the Oval Petals or Leaves on page 22. For a 14x25 pendant bead, use 18 beads for the spine row. Join the wings with square stitch along the diagonal edge at one end. (See Joining Edges with Square Stitch instructions on page 108.) Sew the wing tips and eyes to the hole in the pendant. Hold the wings in place with a drop of glue under each. A bright size 11° seed bead added to each wing tip lends a point of interest.

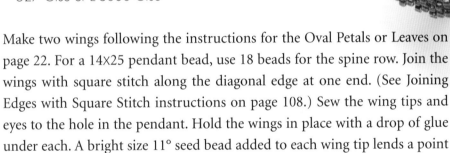

This butterfly was inspired by the Karner blue butterfly, a tiny butterfly with a wingspan no more than 1" (2.5 cm) across. While it can still be found in a few states—Minnesota and Michigan among them—the loss of prairies to farming and land development has led to its decline.

This version is worked with brick stitch. Two pairs of wings are joined and a teardrop bead is added for the body. Once the antennae are formed and sewed in place, they stabilize the wings.

Materials

4 g cylinder beads (Delicas, Treasures, or Aikos)
Teardrop-shaped bead with vertical hole, ¾" (15x8mm) in length
Memory wire, 3" (7.5 cm) piece of 2" (5 cm) diameter wire
Pin back, optional: 1¼" (3.2 cm)

Tools

Round-nose pliers
Memory wire cutter

Upper Wing (Figure 1, make 2)

Thread a needle with 1½ yd (137 cm) of single thread and work brick stitch 2 cylinder beads tall as described below.

Rows 1 and 2: String on 6 beads. Go back through the first 2 beads. Place the beads so they form a T, then tie the working thread to the tail (Figure 3).

Add 2 beads and go up through the last 2 beads added in the previous step (Figure 4).

Add 2 beads and go back through the 2 beads added in the previous step (Figure 5). Continue adding 2 beads and going back through the last 2 beads added until you have four stacks across the bottom and five stacks

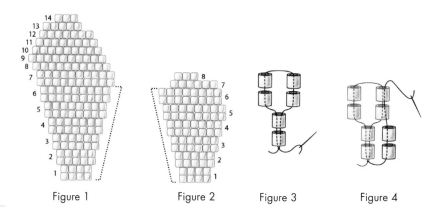

Figure 1   Figure 2   Figure 3   Figure 4

across the top.

Knot the thread between the beads and pass the thread back up through the last stacks of beads in Rows 1 and 2 so you are ready to begin Row 3 (Figure 6). Turn work so you are working left to right.

Row 3: Add 4 beads and catch the first loop. Go back up through the last 2 beads (Figure 7). Work three brick stitches and increase one in the last loop (Figure 8.) There should be six stacks across Row 3.

Rows 4–7: Continue as in Row 3, adding one more stack to each row. Row 7 has ten stacks across.

Row 8: *Note:* Stacks for remaining rows are only 1 bead tall. Add 2 beads and catch the second loop. Go back up through the last bead (Figure 9). Lock the stitch (see Locking the Stitch in Brick Stitch Basics on page 105). Work seven brick stitches and increase one in the last loop—ten stacks across.

Row 9: Add 2 beads and catch the first loop. Go back up through the last bead. Work eight brick stitches—ten stacks across.

Row 10: Add 2 beads and catch the second loop. Go back up through the last bead; lock the stitch. Work seven brick stitches—nine stacks across.

Row 11: Add 2 beads and catch the second loop. Go back up through the last bead; lock the stitch. Work six brick stitches—eight stacks across.

Row 12: Add 2 beads and catch the second loop. Go back up though the last bead; lock the stitch. Work five brick stitches—seven stacks across.

Row 13: Add 2 beads and catch the second loop. Go back up through the last bead; lock the stitch. Work three brick stitches—five stacks across.

Row 14: Add 2 beads and catch the second loop. Go back up through the last bead; lock the stitch. Work one brick stitch—three stacks across. Knot the thread and weave in the tail.

Lower Wing (Figure 2, make 2)

For the first lower wing, use 1 yd (90 cm) of single thread. For the second lower wing, use 2 yd (180 cm) of thread so that you have enough thread to join each pair of upper and lower wings, join the pairs of wings, and add the body and antennae.

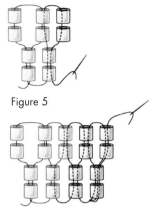

Figure 5

Figure 6

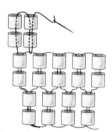

Figure 7

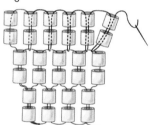

Figure 8

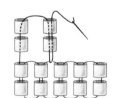

Figure 9

Figure 10

Rows 1–5: Work as for Upper Wing. Row 5 has eight stacks across.

Row 6: Continue with stacks 2 beads tall. Add 4 beads and catch the first loop. Go back up through the last 2 beads. Work six brick stitches—eight stacks across.

Row 7: *Note:* Stacks in the remaining rows are 1 bead tall. Add 2 beads and catch the second loop. Go back up through the last bead; lock the stitch. Work four brick stitches—six stacks across.

Row 8: Add 2 beads and catch the second loop. Go back up through the last bead; lock the stitch. Work one brick stitch. Knot the thread, then use it to sew the wings together—three stacks across.

Joining Upper Wing and Lower Wing

Continue with the thread used for the Lower Wing. Pass the thread through the beads so that it comes out of Row 6 as shown in Figure 10. With square stitch, sew Rows 1–6 of the Upper Wing to Rows 1–6 of the Lower Wing along the sides indicated by the dotted line in Figures 1 and 2. See Figure 10 for square stitch thread path.

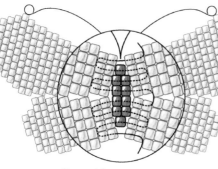

Figure 11

Join the Sets of Wings

Pass the thread to the center bottom of the butterfly wings as shown in Figure 11. Weave the 2 sets of wings together, adding beads as shown to fill the gap between the wings.

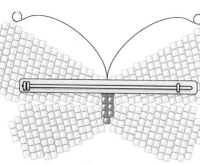

Figure 12

Body

Continuing with the thread used to join the wings, sew the body bead to the center of the wings. Go through the body bead, catch the thread between the beads where they connect at the bottom of the wings, then go back through the body bead. Catch the thread at the top of the joined area, then go back through the body bead. Continue going back and forth until the body is secure. End at the top of the body and you are ready to add the antennae.

Antennae

Bend a 3" (7.5 cm) length of memory wire in the center to form the antennae. With a memory-wire cutter, cut the wire two bead-lengths longer than needed to reach from the center bend to the outermost bead on the upper wing. Bend each end upward to form a loop. Continuing with the thread used to join the wings, sew the center of the antennae to the thread between the wings. Weave the thread through the beads and sew the loops of the antennae to each outermost bead as shown (Figure 12).

For a Pin

Position a pin back as shown in Figure 12 and sew it to the back of the butterfly.

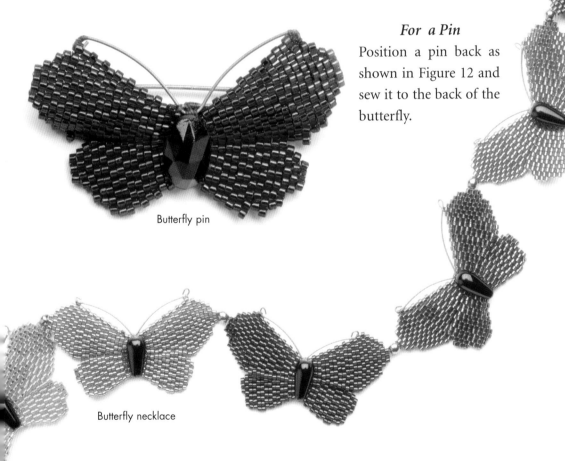

Butterfly pin

Butterfly necklace

Butterfly Necklace
Seven Butterflies are joined at the wing tips with a small round bead between them.

DRAGONFLY WITH A WIRE ARMATURE

Myths about dragonflies are told to children in many cultures, and these predatory insects have many informal names. As a child growing up in the Midwest, I recall my sister telling me that dragonflies were called "sewer-uppers" because they would sew your lips closed. In other parts of the country the insects are referred to as mosquito hawks or "skeeter hawks"; some people call them devil's darning needles for their long, slender body. Dragonflies' delicate wings glisten in the sunlight as they dart about, and their huge bulbous eyes give them a menacing appearance. Add one to your beaded garden. For inspiration, visit www.dragonflies.org.

Materials

For body:

1¼" (3.2 cm) paper clip

1" (2.5 cm) of ½" (1.3 cm) wide paper tape or cloth tape

5 g size 14° seed beads

Sewing thread to match beads

For eyes:

2 size 6° black seed beads, silver/lined or black, or two ¼" (6mm) shank buttons

For wings:

Sheet of transparency copying paper

Optional for iridescent, sparkly wings: Embossing ink and embossing powder in Transparent Kaleidoscope color or other color (both made by Stamp-n Stuff of Newport Beach, California, and used for rubber stamping); and an embossing heat tool

Tools

Flat-nose pliers

Paper scissors

Body

Straighten the narrow end of the paper clip and bend the wider end so it meets the wire to form the head (see Figure 1). Insert a piece of tightly rolled paper or cloth tape in the loop formed for the head. Wrap the rolled tape and the wire carefully with sewing thread to hold the tape roll in place and cover the wire. Wrap several layers of thread around the head to form a base for sewing on the eyes.

Thread a needle with 2½ yd (299 cm) of single thread, add 8 seed beads and tie to form a ring. (Leave 1 yd [90 cm] of thread to bead the tail end.) Slide the ring on the thread-covered wire as far as it will go toward the head. Bead the head with increasing peyote stitch (see page 106). Decrease at the end of the head to completely cover the armature. Thread the tail in the needle and work peyote stitch over the remainder of the body, decreasing as necessary toward the end of the tail.

Wings

On a photocopier, use transparency paper to copy the wings shown in Figure 2. Coat the wing area with embossing ink and sift embossing powder evenly over the ink. Heat with an embossing heat tool, following manufacturer's directions. Cut out the wings and sew to the body.

Eyes

With thread exiting the head, add a size 6° and size 14° bead, go back through the size 6° and stitch into the head. Add the second eye the same way. If you're using small buttons, sew them to the head.

Figure 1

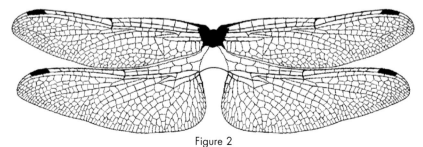

Figure 2

Wing design by Maureen Malloy

SMALL DRAGONFLY

Materials for a pair of earrings

Two 30mm bugles for the bodies
Eight 15mm dagger beads for the wings
4 size 6° seed beads for eyes
2 size 11° seed beads for tails
2 hook-type earring findings
Watch-crystal cement or clear nail polish

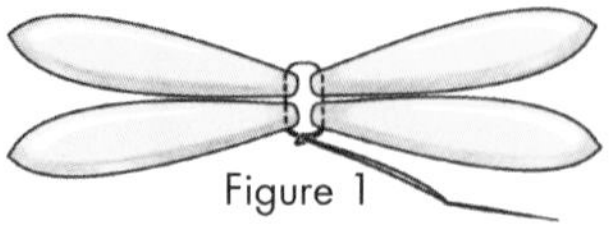

Wings

Step 1. Thread a needle with 1 yd (91.5 cm) of thread. Bring the ends together and knot. Clip the tail close to the knot and melt the knot with a lighter. Wax the thread. String on 4 dagger beads and push them close to the knot. Separate the two strands of thread between the knot and the last bead and pass the needle between the strands, forming a lark's head knot. Position the dagger beads in two pairs across from each other like wings with the needle coming out at the bottom between the pairs (Figure 1). Keep thread tension tight at all times.

Step 2. Pass the needle through the two wings on the left (as shown in Figure 2).

Step 3. With the wings on top of the bugle body, lash the wings to the bugle bead by passing the thread under the bugle, then through the 2 dagger beads on the right going toward the tail (Figure 3).

Step 4. Go under the bugle on the tail side and through the left wings toward the head (Figure 4). Repeat Steps 3 and 4 once more.

Figure 1

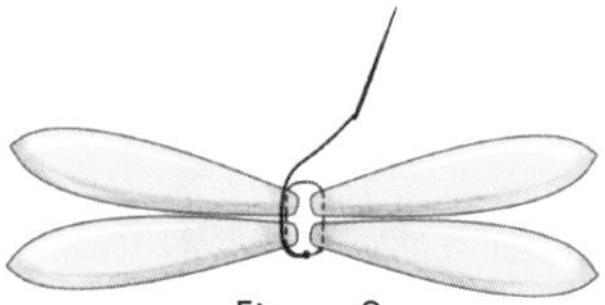

Figure 2

Figure 3

Figure 4

Secure the Wings

Coming out of the left pair of wings with the thread toward the head, go over the bugle and under the right wings. Continue over the bugle and under the left wings. Repeat this step. Go through left wings again, knot the thread, and go through the right wings to bury the tail. Clip off the ends. Position the wings ¼" (6 mm) from the head. Coat the thread on the top and underside of the bugle with watch-crystal cement or clear nail polish to keep the wings from slipping along the bugle.

Figure 5

Figure 6

Add the Eyes and Tail

With thread prepared as in Step 1, string on the 2 size 6° seed beads, secure them side by side with the lark's head knot (see Step 1 and Figure 6), and then go through the bugle. Use care drawing the thread through the bugles—they can be sharp! Add a seed bead and then go back through the bugle (Figure 7). Go through the right eye and then back through the left eye and through the bugle. Position the eyes so they are centered on the bugle body. Repeat going through the eyes and body once. Repeat again and, as you do so, attach an earring finding to the dragonfly finding as follows: Coming out of the right eye, go through the earring finding, then back through the left eye (Figure 8). Knot the thread between the eyes and body and bury the tail in the bugle. Coat all exposed thread with clear nail polish or watch-crystal cement.

Figure 7

Figure 8

This caterpillar is made with what is basically even-count tubular peyote with four sides. One side is the top of the caterpillar, one is the bottom, and two are the sides. The top and bottom are three-drop peyote and the sides are one-drop. The top has stripes that alternate between three seed beads and one 3mm bead. The bottom has stripes that alternate between two colors of seed beads. Even-count tubular peyote requires that at the end of each row you jump up to begin the next row by going through the first bead(s) added for that row.

To MAKE IT EASIER:

• Work counterclockwise
• Check off rows as you work so you don't lose your place
• Keep tension tight
• Lay out beads and label the piles
• Use a Post-it note to indicate your place

Materials

5 g size 11° black seed beads, for the top and bottom stripes

5 g size 11° seed beads (any color except black) for the sides

5 g size 11° seed beads (contrasting color) for the bottom stripe

14 size 11° seed beads for the feet

14 size 8° seed beads for the legs

Ten 3mm round beads for the back

One 4mm round bead for the head

Note: Choose thread to match the side beads.

Step 1. *Prepare the Thread*

Thread a needle with 3 yd (274.5 cm) of thread. Bring the ends together and knot. Clip the tail close to the knot and melt the knot slightly. Wax the thread thoroughly so the strands stick together.

Step 2. *Form the Head*

Add 4 black beads and one 4mm. Push them to within 1" (2.4 cm) of the knot. Part the pair of threads between the black beads and the knot and pass the needle between the strands.

Go back through the 4mm bead. Add 4 black beads. Go through the 4mm and through the first set of 4 black beads.

You now have a 4mm bead with two sets of 4 black seed beads surrounding it. The thread should be coming out of the first set of 4 black beads on the

LARK'S HEAD KNOT BEGINNING

To eliminate weaving in two thread tails when you work with double thread, you may wish to start with a lark's head or sales tag knot. Place an overhand knot in the end of your thread, clip the tail close to the knot, then melt the knot slightly by placing it *near* the base of a lighter flame—it is not necessary to put the knot into the flame. Test the knot by pulling it between your thumb and your index fingernail.

Figure 1

String on the required number of beads and pass them to within 1" (2.5 cm) of the knot. Separate the strands of thread between the knot and the beads and pass the needle between the strands (Figure 1). Draw the thread tight, then go through the first bead next to the knot in the opposite direction (Figure 2). Do not let the knot slip into a bead.

You may also use this method with a single bead or when you use thread single. Begin with the thread double, work for a few stitches, and then clip one of the threads near where they exit a bead.

Figure 2

SEWING OVERLAPPING PETALS TOGETHER

To join two petals that overlap, position as appropriate and hold in place with your fingers. With thread anchored in one of the petals, sew them together with a running stitch as follows: Poke the needle between the beads of both layers, go through a bead in the layer you exit, then poke the needle between the beads to the opposite layer and go through a bead in that layer. Continue as needed.

JOINING EDGES WITH SQUARE STITCH

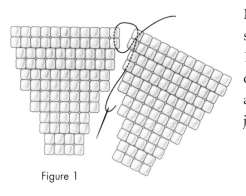

Figure 1

Many of the flowers in this book have petals that join at the edge near the stem end. I recommend joining petals with square stitch as shown in Figure 1. With the thread exiting a bead on the first edge, go through 1 or 2 beads on the edge of the second petal, then through the beads on the first petal again plus the next beads along the edge. Continue like this until the edge is joined.

SQUARE KNOT

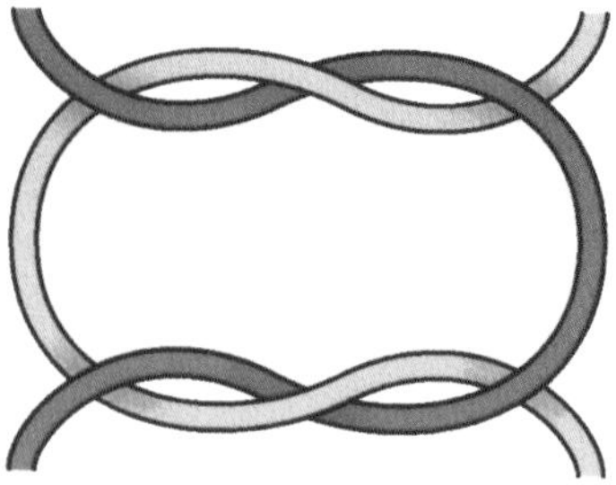

Figure 2

You may use a square knot when you add new thread. Pass the thread through 5–6 beads so that both threads are exiting a bead in the same direction. Bring the right thread over the left thread and pass through the loop. Now the right thread is on the left. Bring the thread on the left over the right thread and pass through the loop.

A GALLERY OF INSPIRATION

Jo Lessa Willey, Fair Oaks, California.
Flower samples, pin. 8–10½" (20.5–26.5 cm) L.
Seed-bead buds on single stems.

Peggy Sturman Gordon, New York, New York.
Wedding Flowers. 10" (25.5 cm) L.
Seed beads with fringe detail in an antique palette.

Alois Powers, St. Paul, Minnesota.
Dreams of Summer When It Is 40 Degrees Below Zero. 15 × 15"
(38 × 38 cm).
Solid seed-bead blooms encircling a necklace.

Margo Field, Albuquerque, New Mexico.
Floral lariat. 111" (281.9 cm) L.
A vine of seed-bead flowers and leaves.

Shelley Bond, Belmont, California.
Outbreak. 30" (76 cm) L; flower 8" (20.5 cm)
Bead-embellished tree branch.

Diane Fitzgerald, Minneapolis, Minnesota.
Tussy Mussy. 8" (20.5 cm) high in vase.
Seed-bead bouquet.

BIBLIOGRAPHY

BEADED FLOWERS

Allen, Mary Lou. "Sunflowers" *Bead & Button Beaddreams*, Special Issue No. 2, 2004.

Bateman, Sharon. *The Morning Rose*. Rathdrum, Idaho: Sharon Bateman, 2001.

Franklin, Kim Z. "Leaves, Petals and Flowers." *Step by Step Beads*, Summer 2003, Vol. 1, No. 2, p. 15.

Grainger, Barbara. *Dimensional Flowers, Leaves & Vines*. Oregon City, Oregon: Barbara L. Grainger, 2000.

Katz, Marcia. *Sculptural Flowers—I. The Trumpet Flower*. Jensen Beach, Florida: Marcia Katz Designs, 2000.

Konstantinov, Varvara. *My Beaded Garden*. Kostroma, Russia: Jewelry by Varvara, 2003.

FLOWER BOOKS

Bessette, Alan E., and William K. Chapman, eds. *Plants and Flowers: 1,761 Illustrations for Artists and Designers*. New York: Dover Publications, 1992.

Biddle, Steve and Megumi. *Handmade Flowers from Paper and Fabric*. Devon, England: David & Charles, 1991.

Gaber, Susan. *Treasury of Flower Designs for Artists, Embroiderers & Craftsmen*. Mineola, New York: Dover Publications, 1981.

Kleinman, Kathryn, and Sara Slavin. *On Flowers*. San Francisco: Chronical Books, 1992.

Laufer, Geraldine Adamich. *Tussie Mussies: The Language of Flowers*. New York: Workman Publishing, 1993.

Palmer, Heather. "Recapturing the Garden," *PieceWork*, May/June, 1999.

Rosart, Sharyn, ed. *Pansies.* New York: Michael Friedman Publishing Group, 2000.

Rosenfeld, Richard. *Perennials.* New York: DK Publishing, 2003.

Scoble, Gretchen, and Ann Field. *The Meaning of Flowers.* San Francisco: Chronicle Books, 1998.

Simmons, Karen. *Painting Flowers in Watercolor.* Mineola, New York: Dover Publications, 1995.

Tolley, Emelie, and Chris Mead. *A Potpourri of Pansies.* New York: Clarkson Potter Publishers, 1993.

Zim, Herbert S. *Flowers: A Golden Guide.* New York: Golden Books, 1987.

LEAVES

Conder, Susan. *Variegated Leaves: The Encyclopedia of Patterned Foliage.* New York: Macmillan Publishing, 1993.

Vitale, Alice Thomas. *Leaves in Myth, Magic and Medicine.* New York: Stewart, Tabori & Chang, 1997.

INDEX

Page numbers in **bold** indicate instructions.
Entries in *italics* indicate pieces by the author using elements described in the book.

The art and craft of beadwork

Books dedicated to building your skills and to fueling your creativity

Beadwork Creates™ Series

Edited by Jean Campbell,
founding editor of *Beadwork* magazine

Dazzle everyone with beautiful hand-beaded bracelets, necklaces, bags, rings, and beaded beads. Learn simple stringing, loomwork, peyote stitch, and other techniques as you create stylish jewelry.

Beadwork Creates Bracelets
ISBN: 1-931499-20-9, paperback
$16.95

Beadwork Creates Necklaces
ISBN: 1-931499-22-5, paperback
$16.95

Beadwork Creates Beaded Beads
ISBN: 1-931499-27-6, paperback
$16.95

Beadwork Creates Beaded Bags
ISBN: 1-931499-34-9, paperback
$16.95

Beadwork Creates Beaded Rings
ISBN: 1-931499-26-8, paperback
$16.95

Beadwork Creates Earrings
ISBN: 1-931499-61-6, paperback
$16.95

INTERWEAVE PRESS®
201 East Fourth Street • Loveland, Colorado 80537-5655